ON THE
ILLINOIS FRONTIER

Dr. Hiram⌊Rutherford

1840–1848

Edited by

WILLENE HENDRICK
GEORGE HENDRICK

Southern Illinois University Press
Carbondale and Edwardsville
1981

Copyright © 1982 by Southern Illinois University Press
All rights reserved
Printed in the United States of America
Edited by Rosemary Yeagle
Designed by Quentin Fiore
Production supervised by Richard Neal

LIBRARY OF CONGRESS CATALOGING IN PUBLICATION DATA

Rutherford, Hiram.
   On the Illinois frontier.

   (Medical humanities series)
   Bibliography: p.
   Includes index.
   1. Rutherford, Hiram. 2. Physicians—Illinois—
Coles Co.—Correspondence. 3. Frontier and pioneer
life—Illinois—Coles Co.—Sources. 4. Coles Co.,
Ill.—History—19th century—Sources. I. Hendrick,
Willene, 1928-   . II. Hendrick, George.
III. Title. IV. Series.
R154.R87A36   610'.9773'72   80-28651
ISBN 0-8093-0990-4

For Sarah
A pioneer in her own right

CONTENTS

ILLUSTRATIONS

PREFACE

One Sunday morning in the late summer of 1977, we learned from an Urbana, Illinois, newspaper that the nineteenth-century home of Dr. Hiram Rutherford was being maintained as a museum by Landmarks, Inc. (a local historical society in Oakland, a farming community near Urbana). From reading Carl Sandburg's biography of Lincoln, we knew that Dr. Rutherford had been one of Lincoln's acquaintances but that their friendship had cooled after the celebrated *Matson* slave trial of 1847. General Robert Matson, a Kentucky planter, brought his slaves up from Bourbon County, Kentucky, to work his farm near Oakland each summer. Five slaves, fearing they might be sold down the river, placed themselves under the protection of Gideon Matthew Ashmore, a hotelkeeper, and Dr. Rutherford, both Abolitionists. Matson then sued Dr. Rutherford and Ashmore for harboring fugitive slaves. Dr. Rutherford asked Lincoln to represent him and the slaves, but Lincoln had already agreed to represent Matson. Dr. Rutherford and Ashmore hired other lawyers, won the case, and the slaves were freed, but Dr. Rutherford never again wholeheartedly admired Lincoln.

When we visited Rutherford House that Sunday, our guide was Helen Parkes, editor of the Oakland *Ledger-Messenger* and one of the founders of Landmarks, Inc. During the tour we asked Mrs. Parkes whether the doctor had left papers of historical interest, and she told us that Dr. Rutherford's descendants had indeed preserved many of his papers. She had copies of some of his letters, which she let us borrow. With her help in the weeks that followed, we met members of the Rutherford family and were able to see and copy other letters by Rutherford, the doctor's medical ledger, and the lecture notes he took when he was a student at Jefferson Medical College in Philadelphia from 1836 to 1838. In addition, we found copies of a dozen evocative articles by Dr. Rutherford about life on the Illinois frontier. Only one of these articles, Dr. Rutherford's account of the old frontiersman John Richman, whom Mark Van Doren used as his central character in *The Mayfield Deer*, was previously known to a large audience. We also located new materials concerning the *Matson* trial.

This work would not have been possible without the help of Dr. Rutherford's descendants—Harriet Rutherford Crawford, the late Eugenia Rutherford Nichols, Cyrus Rutherford Nichols, Janet Nichols Bass, Austin Rutherford, and Nina Rutherford Zimmerman—who have been unfailingly generous in providing iformation and making available family papers and books. We also wish to acknowledge our indebtedness to Helen Parkes, who first introduced us to the Rutherford heritage and made the resources of the Rutherford home available to us.

George Hendrick is indebted to Dean Emeritus Robert W. Rogers and Director Daniel Alpert for their many kindnesses during the past years.

Grants from the Research Board of the University of Illinois and Friends of Medical Humanities, Southern Illinois University, helped make possible the publication of this volume.

WILLENE HENDRICK
GEORGE HENDRICK

Urbana, Illinois
December 1980

INTRODUCTION

Dr. Hiram Rutherford, a young physician and surgeon, left his native Pennsylvania late in 1840 to seek his fortune in a newly settled part of eastern Illinois. He set up practice in Oakland (at that time commonly called Independence), during the last weeks of the year, and he remained in that village until his death in 1900. He did indeed succeed in the West, and though he did not seek fame, he played an historical role in Lincoln's life and is remembered today as a man of principle aligned with the Abolitionists in the *Matson* slave case. He married twice, both times happily, and reared eight children who survived infancy. He acquired land and goods and prospered mightily, but he did not ignore the public good: as school treasurer he did much to support public education; he served on many village and county government boards; and he was untiring in tending to his medical practice. During his early years in Illinois he wrote vivid and enthusiastic letters back to Pennsylvania describing his experiences in his new life, and after retirement from his profession in the late 1870s he wrote a spirited series of articles about life on the Illinois frontier of the 1840s. He was, then, more than just an ordinary Illinois country doctor.

Hiram Rutherford was born near Harrisburg, Pennsylvania, in 1815. His Scotch-Irish great-grandfather, Thomas Rutherford, had emigrated from Ireland to America in 1729. Thomas's son John served as an officer in the Revolutionary army. John's son William was Hiram's father. They were a good family, a solid family, but they were not wealthy. Hiram was the eighth child, and he was, as he said, "raised to heavy farm labor." It is likely, then, that he could not be spared for school many months a year. He attended what is sometimes called a "blab school"— there was much "blabber" in the one room—and young Rutherford learned to go about his own work oblivious to the noise around him. He was to retain this power of concentration the rest of his life. He also developed a taste for reading, especially history and historical novels, the latter interest perhaps influenced by the traditional family belief that the Rutherfords were distantly related to Sir Walter Scott.[1]

At the age of eighteen Hiram Rutherford left the family home in Paxtang, Pennsylvania, and began to study medicine with an older brother, William, who was already a medical doctor with an established practice in nearby Harrisburg. It is unlikely that young Hiram had graduated from an academy. Before the Civil War educational prerequisites for studying medicine were scanty. Three years of apprenticeship (not high school or college) were generally required before students could enter medical school. Dr. Rutherford did not leave an account of this period of his life, but William Frederick Norwood, in his standard history, *Medical Education in the United States Before the Civil War*, has this to say: "The duties of a young man . . . were numerous. He learned to make pills, mix potions and powders, cup, bleed, and do bedside nursing. Not a few of these half-fledged youths were also expected to act as sweep and stable boy for the doctor."[2] Normally, the apprentice paid a fee of one hundred dollars a year to the physician, but it is unlikely that Hiram Rutherford was asked to pay this fee to his physician brother or that he was assigned extensive stable duties. It is reasonable to assume that he spent his time observing and aiding

1. From the family records of Austin Rutherford, the late Eugenia Rutherford Nichols, C. R. Nichols, Nina Rutherford Zimmerman, and Harriet Rutherford Crawford. Dr. Rutherford undoubtedly wrote his own biographical sketch in the *History of Coles County, Illinois*, pp. 576–77, and information from that sketch has been used, as well as Harriet Crawford's sketch of her grandfather in *History of Coles County, 1876–1976*, pp. 823–24. See also *The Spirit of Independence*.

2. William Frederick Norwood, *Medical Education in the United States Before the Civil War*, p. 32.

his brother and reading the medical texts in the office. Apprenticeship was of special importance to young medical students such as Hiram Rutherford, for it was during these years that they saw patients, learned how to make diagnoses, and learned appropriate bedside manner. Medical schools of the 1830s gave almost no clinical instruction—the course of study was confined to lectures and anatomy demonstrations; hospitals were rarely used for teaching.

Hiram Rutherford registered as a student in Jefferson Medical College in Philadelphia on November 9, 1836.[3] The young man chose his college well, for Jefferson had one of the most distinguished faculties in the United States. Jefferson Medical College was founded by Dr. George McClellan in 1825. The new school was in direct competition for students with the well-established University of Pennsylvania Medical College, also in Philadelphia, and Jefferson Medical College had several difficult years. By the middle 1830s, however, Dr. McClellan was able to bring together a remarkably able faculty, including himself as Professor of Surgery; Dr. John Revere, son of Paul Revere, as Professor of Principles and Practice of Physic; Dr. Granville Sharp Pattison as Professor of Anatomy; and Dr. Robley Dunglison as Professor of the Institutes of Medicine and Medical Jurisprudence. Competent people also filled the chairs of Chemistry, Materia Medica, and Midwifery and Diseases of Women and Children.[4]

Biographical data affords a fairly clear picture of the distinguished faculty at Jefferson. Dr. McClellan, a graduate of the University of Pennsylvania Medical School, was by all accounts an excellent teacher of surgery. He was a forceful lecturer with a resounding voice, and he commanded the complete attention of his students.[5]

---

3. Information supplied by Robert T. Lentz, Archivist, Thomas Jefferson University, Philadelphia.

4. *Annual Announcement of Lectures, &c. in Jefferson Medical College, for the Session of 1837–8*; Norwood, pp. 86–93. See also Edward Louis Bauer, *Doctors Made in America.*

5. Bauer, pp. 4–5. Dr. McClellan's son, George Brinton, was a general in the Union army and Democratic candidate for the presidency in 1864.

Dr. John Revere seems to have worn his father's fame with ease. John Revere graduated from Harvard and then took his medical degree at Edinburgh. He was the editor of the *Medical Record* and apparently a fine lecturer. "In his lectures," according to one student, "he always laid out his ground with great care, kept his subject carefully before him and presented it as a connected whole after a method so severe and exact that a student who would give it his undivided attention could not fail to receive important instruction."[6]

Dr. Pattison was a graduate of the University of Glasgow, Scotland.[7] He was a master teacher, according to this statement in his biographical sketch: "It is probable that no anatomical teacher of his time attained a higher reputation. His reputation lay in his knowledge of visceral and surgical anatomy, and in the practical application of this knowledge to the diagnosis and treatment of disease, accidents, and operations. His earnest manner and clever demonstrations made him very popular in the lecture room." Alfred Stillé wrote of Dr. Pattison's showmanship: "I shall never forget his lecture upon the skull, in which he recited with admirable feeling [while undoubtedly holding a skull in his hand] the famous lines of Byron beginning 'Is this a place where a god might dwell?'"[8]

In his youth, Robley Dunglison studied Latin and Greek, mathematics, and English grammar. By the time he began his study of medicine, he no doubt had well-developed logical and

6. Ibid., p. 32. See the biographical sketch of Dr. Revere in Howard A. Kelly and Walter L. Burrage, *American Medical Biographies*, p. 972.

7. Dr. Pattison was not only a remarkable teacher of anatomy but also a man with a colorful past. He left Scotland after being named corespondent in a divorce case. Although he was exonerated, the charges against him were well known. He came to America in 1818 thinking he had been promised the Chair of Anatomy at the University of Pennsylvania Medical School, but that appointment did not materialize. Dr. Nathaniel Chapman of that school opposed Dr. Pattison's appointment on moral grounds; the two argued bitterly, and Dr. Pattison fought a duel with Dr. Chapman's brother-in-law, General Thomas Cadwalader. Fortunately for the sake of medical education, Dr. Pattison was uninjured, though "a ball passed through the skirt of his coat near the waist." Kelly and Burrage, p. 896.

8. Ibid., p. 896; Bauer, p. 35.

analytical faculties. He studied medicine in Edinburgh, Paris, and London, and received his surgical degree in 1819 from the Royal College of Surgeons and his medical degree in 1823 from Erlangen. In 1824, Thomas Jefferson, who was devoting himself to developing the University of Virginia, brought Dr. Dunglison to Charlottesville. This was one of Jefferson's more inspired appointments, for Dr. Dunglison was one of the most important medical educators of his time. Concerning Dunglison's book *Human Physiology*, originally published in 1832, Dr. S. D. Gross wrote, "What Haller's great work accomplished for surgery in the eighteenth century, Dunglison accomplished for physiology in America in the nineteenth century." Dr. Dunglison's *Medical Dictionary*, published in 1833, sold 55,000 copies in his lifetime. He also wrote such influential books as *Materia Medica, Hygiene,* and *The Practice of Medicine*. In all, 120,000 copies of his books were sold—very high sales indeed for the nineteenth century, and indicative of his influence on a generation of American medical students. In addition, Dr. Dunglison was physician to Jefferson, Madison, Monroe, and Jackson—certainly a list to impress his students and colleagues.[9] Dr. Dunglison's acceptance of a chair at Jefferson Medical College in 1836 greatly enhanced the reputation of the Philadelphia college.

It is clear, then, that Hiram Rutherford had enrolled in a prestigious medical school with an outstanding faculty, many of whose members were Scottish-trained. That in itself gave the school added prestige, for Scotland at that time was a major medical center in the Western world. We also know what the young medical student studied in his two years at Jefferson, for many of his college texts and his notebooks have survived.[10] The medical books which he owned during his college days included the following: John Hunter's *A Treatise on the Blood, Inflammation, and Gun-Shot Wounds* (1817); Sam'l Cooper's *The First Lines of the Practice of Surgery* (1835); John Eberle's *A Treatise on the Practice of Medicine* (1838); Samuel Sheldon Fitch's *A System of Dental Surgery* (1835); John and Charles Bell's *The Anatomy and Physiology*

9. Kelly and Burrage, pp. 342–43; Bauer, pp. 50–55.
10. The notebooks are on microfilm in the University of Illinois Library. The original texts are also in the library.

of the Human Body (1834); and Robley Dunglison's *Human Physiology* (1836). Soon after Rutherford completed his medical training, he purchased Hall's *The Principles of Diagnosis* (1839), and over the years he built up a small personal medical library.[11]

Hiram Rutherford was obviously a serious student. His notebooks show that he attended lectures regularly and took careful notes. Judging from their clarity and legibility, he perhaps meticulously recopied them each night. His notes show that he was practical minded. When Dr. Dunglison gave a prescription to relieve constipation, Rutherford carefully copied down the ingredients for later use in his own practice.

Most of the lectures which he heard were not theoretical; they concentrated on practical matters: how to lance a boil, how to perform a specific surgical procedure. Only minor attention was paid to classical theories. For instance, Dr. Revere began one lecture with a discussion of Galen and the four humors, but Dr. Revere did not accept those designations, preferring instead to talk of constitutions, and spending most of his lecture describing neurotics whose minor afflictions were difficult to cure. He also discussed patients prone to tuberculosis, giving precise descriptions of those suffering from this disease: their flat chests, stumpy fingers, pale skins. He observed sagely, given the state of medicine in the 1830s, that remedies had little effect on those suffering from consumption.[12]

When Hiram Rutherford entered Jefferson Medical College in 1836, students were expected to attend two full courses of lectures. Each course was four months long, from November 1 to March 1. The faculty had difficulty in covering their subjects in the allotted time and added an additional month of lectures in October, but this session was optional. Fees (paid directly to the professor) were fifteen dollars for each lecture subject. Hiram Rutherford paid fees to seven professors, ten dollars for the use of the dissecting room, and five dollars for museum and dispensary fees. His fees for each four-month course would have been $120; to the $240 he would have paid for two years

11. Rutherford materials, University of Illinois Library.
12. Ibid.

of classes was added a graduation fee of twenty dollars, for a total of $260. In addition he had to pay the cost of his books and his living expenses in Philadelphia.[13]

At the end of his second session, he submitted a dissertation on "Dropsy" and was examined by the professors. In the spring of 1838, along with 107 others, he became a graduate of Jefferson Medical College and a medical doctor ready to practice.[14]

Dr. Hiram Rutherford left Philadelphia with ten dollars, a horse, saddle, and bridle. At twenty-three, with angular good looks and a strong desire to succeed, he was entering practice during the severe economic depression which followed the Panic of 1837. He settled first in Millersburg, Pennsylvania, not far from his parents' home, but he remained there for only two years—two frustrating years. There were many other doctors in that area, and it soon became clear to him that it would be exceedingly difficult for a poor young man to establish a practice. During this time, though, he met a young lady, Lucinda Bowman, with whom he fell in love. When the young doctor began to see that he would not prosper in Millersburg, he determined to move West. Doctors were scarce on the frontier, and he knew that his chances of building a practice were better in a newly settled area. He seems to have thought he was too poor to marry, but Lucinda, a high-spirited girl, seems not to have agreed, for she would not write to him after he moved West. What Dr. Rutherford did not know when he departed for Illinois was that Lucinda's mother was bitterly opposed to the idea of her daughter moving with him to the "unhealthy" West.

In the late fall of 1840, young Dr. Rutherford and two other young physicians, who had been his classmates, left Pennsylvania for "Illenois" (as he spelled and undoubtedly pronounced it). Their trip on horseback was uneventful, and all three settled in the east central part of the state. Dr. Rutherford cast his lot with Independence (later renamed Oakland) in Coles County. That area had been settled in 1829, but when Dr. Rutherford

13. *Annual Announcement of Lectures, &c. in Jefferson Medical College, for the Session of 1837–8.*

14. Robert T. Lentz provided us with the title of Dr. Rutherford's dissertation; the number of Jefferson graduates for 1838 is in Norwood, p. 89.

arrived it was still sparsely populated and the prairie lands had hardly been touched. One other physician ("poorly educated," Dr. Rutherford says, implying that the other physician had not attended medical school) was in Oakland, but Dr. Rutherford was newly trained and energetic and began to build a large practice. He brought with him his Jefferson diploma, suitably written in Latin, attesting that Hiram Rutherford was a medical doctor graduated from a reputable college. It is likely that the young man did not hide the eminence of several of his professors—that one was the son of an American hero, and that another had been personal physician to American presidents. Dr. Rutherford had another advantage as he began his practice among the settlers of east central Illinois: he had grown up on a farm and had known hard physical labor. He could understand the frontier people, and they could understand him.

Just what kind of practice did Dr. Rutherford establish in Illinois? He was trained as a "regular" physician; he was not a Thomsonian using botanical remedies, nor was he a homeopath using minute doses.[15] He began his practice during the reign of heroic medicine—the medical discipline which prescribed massive doses of purgatives such as calomel, and held a general belief in the efficacy of cupping, blistering, and bloodletting. Dr. Rutherford's account books show that he seldom resorted to bloodletting, and he did not order from his drug supply company massive amounts of calomel, indicating he was more sparing in his use of heroic measures than many other regular practitioners, though he did try blistering and bloodletting during his wife Lucinda's fatal illness. It is likely that Dr. Rutherford was conservative in his treatments because his professors at Jefferson Medical College did not recommend the most extreme heroic treatments.

There were no nearby drugstores, and he prepared his own medicines from drugs he ordered from Pennsylvania. A receipt for medicines ordered from Gross, a Harrisburg drug company, gives us indirect clues to the kind of medical practice Dr. Ruth-

15. For an excellent account of Thomsonians, homeopaths, and regulars, see William G. Rothstein, *American Physicians in the Nineteenth Century*, and Martin Kaufman, *Homeopathy in America*.

erford had. Gross shipped to him in April of 1842 a large order of drugs and supplies. The bill totalled $66.37½ and included: $2.00 for calomel, $4.00 for opium, $14.00 for quinine (he ordered more, but it was scarce and Gross could not fill the entire order), and $.94 for catheters. In all, Gross sent sixty-five items. From this receipt we can surmise that malaria was the most common disease; Rutherford did use some calomel, as most "regulars" did; he controlled pain with opium; and he used catheters in the removal of kidney stones.

The area of Illinois that Dr. Rutherford covered in his practice was sparsely settled; there were Southerners from border states, other settlers from middle western states to the east of Illinois, some New Englanders, and a few European immigrants. This mixed group of frontierspeople had a host of medical superstitions and beliefs. Because they often lived long distances from a doctor, or could not afford medical attention, or distrusted doctors, most of the pioneers employed home remedies whenever possible. Some of these remedies were European in origin; others were based on Indian herbal medicines. The remedies were passed down from generation to generation and were also published in newspapers and domestic medical books. Many of the remedies were teas made from native plants: peppermint and tansy tea for dysentery, rhubarb bitters for indigestion, catnip tea for pleurisy, and sassafras tea to clean the blood.[16] Poultices were concocted for "chest complaints." There were literally thousands of these home remedies, large numbers of which were undoubtedly of little value in curing the complaint but also less dangerous than massive doses of purgatives or the removal of a quart of blood.

Some of the folk remedies were, however, much more complicated than simple teas and poultices. For gout and rheumatism, a dog oil massage was recommended by Dr. Richard Carter in *Valuable Vegetable Medical Prescriptions for the cure of All Nervous*

16. See the useful chapter "Home Remedies and Domestic Medicine" in Madge E. Pickard and R. Carlyle Buley, *The Midwest Pioneer*; see also J. K. Crellin, "Health and Medicine in Central and Southern Pioneer Illinois," (unpublished manuscript available through Department of Medical Humanities, Southern Illinois University School of Medicine, Springfield, Illinois), pp. 25–30.

and Putrid Disorders: "Take a young fat dog and kill him, scald and clean him as you would a pig, then extract his guts through a hole previously made in his side, and substitute in the place thereof, two handfuls of nettles, two ounces of brimstone, one dozen hen eggs, four ounces of turpentine, a handful of tanzy, a pint of red fishing worms, and about three-fourths of a pound of tobacco, cut up fine; mix all those ingredients well together before [they are] deposited in the dogs belly, and then sew up the whole, then roast him well before a hot fire, save the oil, annoint the joints, and weak parts before the fire as hot as you can bear it, being careful not to get wet or expose yourself to damp or night air, or even heating yourself, or in fact you should not expose yourself in any way."[17] The hot oil and the heat from the fire undoubtedly made the rheumatic sufferer feel considerably better, if he was able to persevere through the long preparation.

If home remedies did not bring relief, the patient then most likely sought out a physician, though his choice in most cases may have been determined by the practitioner's proximity rather than his competence. While some pioneer physicians, like Dr. Rutherford, had attended medical school, others had merely served an apprenticeship, and still others had set themselves up in practive by simply taking the title of "doctor."

Patients were not scarce, for east central Illinois in the 1840s was not the healthiest place in the world. The most common illness in the late summer was malaria. Water stood in puddles on the prairie and small streams were often sluggish; mosquitoes were everywhere. The settlers, indeed the physicians, were unaware of the connection between mosquito and malaria, though Dr. Rutherford could treat the disease, as shown by his large purchases of quinine. During his early years of practice at Oakland, he would have been called upon also to treat many of the following: smallpox, cholera, erysipelas, puerperal fever, scarlet fever, dysentery, infant diarrhea, tuberculosis, pneumonia, influenza, measles, chicken pox, venereal diseases—the

17. Pickard and Buley, pp. 63–64.

list is certainly not complete.[18] The fact that medical science in 1840 did not understand the cause and cure of most of the illnesses listed above is well known. The medicines employed by botanics, homeopaths, and regular physicians alike at that time were often ill-advised or useless. However, it is obvious from his letters that Dr. Rutherford carried on a successful practice in the face of almost universal medical ignorance, unfavorable working conditions, and limited equipment.

During his first years in Illinois, Dr. Rutherford had no regular office. Patients who came into town to see him were examined in his parlor, but more generally he visited them in their homes. Getting into the countryside during blizzards and during rainy seasons was in itself a major undertaking. Dr. Rutherford described part of the problem:

> the practice of medicine in a new country is a work of great labor, when the calls are numerous and the extent of territory covered, as in this case, embraced half a degree of latitude and longitude; the roads at that time were mere deer-paths, and the streams were allowed to flow on their winding to the sea, unvexed by bridges or ferries, except such of the latter as a dug-out canoe afforded; canoe ferriage, now one of the lost arts, was then a distinguished occupation in high-water times; the traveler led his stripped horse in the water on the upper side of the canoe, taking for himself and saddle a position mid-way between the bow and the stern; the ferryman, seated on the stern, paddle in hand, sent the unsteady craft across the stream, carefully keeping pace with the swimming horse; the small streams had to be forded, in which case a high horse was a valuable help, but not unfrequently a glorious dunking was the result of such necessary adventures.[19]

Under such conditions, Dr. Rutherford could carry only the barest equipment and medicines. He would venture out with previously prepared doses of quinine, opium, calomel, and other often-prescribed drugs; splints and bandages; and equip-

18. See Isaac D. Rawlings, *The Rise and Fall of Disease in Illinois*, vol. 1, and Lucius H. Zeuch, *History of Medical Practice in Illinois*, vol. 1.
19. *History of Coles County, Illinois*, p. 577.

ment useful in delivering a baby, removing kidney stones from the bladder, and for such minor surgery as lancing a boil, bloodletting, or extracting a tooth. At his home he had additional equipment: mortar and pestle, scales, bottles and containers of bulk drugs (he compounded all of his own prescriptions, since there was no drug store in his community); his medical texts for reference; and his medical school notes. As Pickard and Buley observe in *The Midwest Pioneer: His Ills, Cures & Doctors,* "In the absence of complicated equipment for diagnosis he [the pioneer doctor] relied upon his fingers, eyes, ears, and nose. Temperature and pulse he could feel; color of skin, lips, eyes, and fingernails meant much, as did the sound of voice, cough, and breathing of the patient. He could smell out a case of typhoid, measles, or milk sickness."[20]

At a later time, Dr. Rutherford built a small office across the street from his home and saw his patients there instead of in his front parlor. When the roads were improved, he was able to travel by buggy into the countryside instead of riding horseback as he did in his early years in Oakland. He was a regular reader of medical journals (he subscribed to *The British and Foreign Medico-Chirurgical Review, American Journal of the Medical Sciences,* and *Half-yearly Abstract of the Medical Sciences*), and he undoubtedly began using new medicines and new surgical equipment as they were introduced into general practice.

We know from his early ledgers that he charged $5.00 to deliver a baby, $2.00 to set a bone, $.50 for a dozen quinine pills. $.25 for bleeding. If patients could not pay in cash, Dr. Rutherford would accept produce or services. One woman did sewing for him; a man who owed him $24.50 worked ten days at $.50 a day and then gave the doctor a note for the rest of the bill.[21] Though his fees were moderate, and his patients did not always pay him in cash, Dr. Rutherford prospered. His practice was large, but his other activities (farming, banking, public service) did not detract unduly from his attention to his patients.

In the three sections which follow, Dr. Rutherford will be seen

20. Pickard and Buley, pp. 99–100.

21. From the account books of Dr. Rutherford, several of which have been placed on loan to the University of Illinois Library.

as a private man experiencing the emotional turmoil resulting from his move to the frontier, and as a physician bringing medical care to a newly settled area. He will be seen as a writer attempting to recapture the people and events which he carefully and sensitively observed in the 1840s. Finally, he will be seen as a humanitarian who played a major role in helping keep five slaves from being returned to servitude. Though fragmentary, these documents, taken as a whole, give us the connected pieces of one remarkable life; they tell us much about early medical practice on the frontier; and they show us something of life among the settlers of one Illinois community from 1840 to 1848.

The Letters

The Letters

We know a great deal about Dr. Rutherford's life during his first years in Illinois because some of his and his wife Lucinda's letters have survived. They are reproduced here just as they were written, with only an occasional mark of punctuation added silently in order to make the meaning clear. Hiram Rutherford and Lucinda Bowman Rutherford were both erratic spellers, and their grammatical structures were sometimes far from standard. They were not graduates of established academies and undergraduate colleges. To alter their letters, however, would be to change these young people. We wish to present them as they were.

Most of the letters were written by Dr. Rutherford to John Bowman, Lucinda's brother. When Dr. Rutherford addressed letters to Lucinda, still in Pennsylvania, he received no answers. Obviously hoping to maintain contact with her, he began to correspond with her brother, who lived in Elizabethville, only a few miles from Millersburg. From his first letter, dated March 10, 1841, Dr. Rutherford was subtly making his case as a suitable suitor for Lucinda: he wrote of his successful medical practice, reporting that his fees were double those he charged in Pennsylvania.

John Bowman was a storekeeper, and Dr. Rutherford wrote in detail about local commerce: merchandise in Independence sold for double the Pennsylvania prices, and groceries were one third higher and could be sold for cash; wheat sold for fifty cents a bushel, corn for twenty cents, and pork for three cents a pound. There were no stores in Independence, previous ones having closed, and Dr. Rutherford urged Bowman to cast his fortunes with the West, too. What the young doctor did not say, but clearly implied, was that he hoped Bowman would move to Independence, bringing Lucinda with him. Since the doctor could not make such an outright admission to Bowman, he simply asked to be remembered to Lucinda.

By July of 1841 Dr. Rutherford was writing even more insistently to John Bowman. (While Dr. Rutherford does not say so, Lucinda was apparently still not responding to his letters.) He wrote about the "Scandalizers" of Millersburg, saying that he was glad to have left that town, for he had fallen into "some ruinous habits" there, vices he hoped to leave off entirely. Given his general character and his devotion to medicine, it is unlikely that he drank heavily in Millersburg; rather, he was reinforcing in his letters his case as a suitable husband for Lucinda—he had given up his bad habits. We learn later that he had taken the temperance pledge.

From the correspondence it is obvious that Dr. Rutherford was beginning to love the West, to know its people, and to enjoy frontier life, though his ties to his family and especially his emotional ties to Lucinda were still strong. He wrote in detail about the growth of his practice and his success in treating scarlet fever and malaria. His life seems to have been one of tremendous labor as he made visits to patients over a wide area, but his work was not enough—his life was incomplete without Lucinda. In the letter of April 27, 1842, he wrote to Bowman that he hoped to return to Millersburg "an independent man" and put "to rights some <u>things</u> which I should never have left wrong."

Most of John Bowman's letters have not survived, but we do have one dated May 13, 1842, and from it we can see that Dr. Rutherford had been too subtle in making his case. Responding to Dr. Rutherford's comment that he had not received replies from Millersburg, John wrote, "If to my Sister Lucinda you wrote, which is only conjecture by me: I can probably guess at it why you received no answer. Delicacy or timidity was doubtless the cause." To this letter, Dr. Rutherford, a young man of twenty-seven, over eighteen months away from Lucinda, replied with considerable exasperation.

The resolution was soon to come, however. John Bowman gave Lucinda Dr. Rutherford's letter of July 31, 1842, and she returned it to her brother. Dr. Rutherford was distressed to learn that Bowman did not argue for the absent suitor, but the doctor pressed his own case by writing to Lucinda once again, a letter sent by way of John. That letter to Lucinda has not survived, but the one to John, dated November 24, 1842, has. In it, Dr. Rutherford spoke of himself as "an exile in a distant land." After saying he was sending along a letter for Lucinda, the doctor announced: "If she should answer me according to my desires I may probably return in 3 months, but certainly in six; if she does not, I do not expect ever to be back, at least not for years yet, and then it will only be at the urgent solicitation of my aged parents." The letter also contains a passage which may well have influenced Lucinda's decision: "I can assure you I might in my opinion connect myself with the fairest, and most wealthy of this land, if my taste did not lead me another way." It is likely that John passed on at least this part of the letter's message to Lucinda.

Lucinda did write, though her letter to the doctor is missing, and the next spring, in April of 1843, the two were married in Pennsylvania. The young couple then returned to Illinois. Lucinda soon wrote to her mother about their trip West, the beauty of the prairies, and the friendliness of the inhabitants of Independence. Dr. Rutherford wrote to his brother-in-law, John Bowman, on October 21, 1843, about setting up housekeeping. He seemed a happy, contented man, after all the frustrations of the past years. He spoke of his practice and of Lucinda's health. "Sickness has been pretty abundant. I have never done so much in one summer before, & yet I have lost but 2 patients in all my practice since my return. In August I booked about $250. I have had good health. Lucinda has had several shakes of the ague, and in August while attending a camp meeting she took cold, and had the fever for two or 3 days, most reverendly." The fever contracted at the Methodist Camp Meeting foreshadowed the tragedy that would befall the young couple at a future camp meeting.

Lucinda's letters to her mother tell how she and the doctor lived. They occupied "about the best house in town, though it is only one story high." She did the milking, for she did not like to see a man doing such work. One of her few criticisms of her new home was that the climate of the West was not as healthy as that of the East. She told her mother about her fever during the summer of 1843, but she did not report that she was pregnant. On June 26, 1844, Dr. Rutherford wrote to his brother-in-law about the birth of John Rutherford. The next year was one of great personal happiness for Hiram and Lucinda. Dr. Rutherford's letters to his brother-in-law were relaxed; he described political and economic conditions in Illinois, spoke of his and Lucinda's pleasures with their young son, and commented on his continuing success as a physician.

The young couple's happiness and their promising future ended abruptly. Dr. Rutherford wrote the details to John Bowman on October 14, 1845. Lucinda, after attending another Methodist Camp Meeting, again became ill with the fever, and died. Despite all his skills as a physician, Dr. Rutherford was unable to save her. He blamed himself for not recognizing the gravity of her illness soon enough, for continuing to see his other patients while his own wife lay critically ill. The letter is a vivid description of her illness, death, and burial—and his own feelings of guilt.

Dr. Rutherford wrote to his mother-in-law about Lucinda's death, and although we do not have the letter, it was probably similar to the one he mailed to John. Mrs. Bowman's response (also missing, but its contents can be surmised from the doctor's reply) caused Dr. Rutherford great distress: she wanted Lucinda's body returned to Pennsylvania; she offered to take the infant John into her own home, away from the unhealthy climate in Illinois; she doubted that the Methodist Camp Meeting contributed to Lucinda's death; and she expressed her long-standing opposition to Lucinda's marriage. Dr. Rutherford declined to remove Lucinda's body; he did not wish to part with his son; and he wrote Mrs. Bowman about the effects of her opposition to the marriage. "You say you are all verry sorry that you let her leave you. On that point you should not reflect upon yourselves, you could not prevent it, I was never aware till the day of her death, how much you opposed her going with me. At that time, when I first saw the reality of her situation, I burst into tears. She spoke to me in all the sweetness of her nature. 'Honey I beleive I must die.' . . . She then added 'Mother told me before we married, that I would follow you and loose my own soul.' . . . To die so far from her people was as you say distressing. Her who had pronounced the curse which lay upon her soul, was not with her to remoove the load." This statement has in it the immediacy and passion of much of the great literature of the nineteenth century.

The next months were lonely ones for Dr. Rutherford, though they were undoubtedly made more bearable by his young son, who stayed in good health, and by the extensive medical work which took most of his time. He sent his son to live with a woman in the neighborhood, and for a time he continued to live in the house he had shared with Lucinda. He had always loved the wild roses which grew in profusion around Independence, and he planted some of them around Lucinda's grave. He continued to correspond with John Bowman. He sent Bowman pressed flowers from Lucinda's grave, and he kept Bowman informed about the health of John Rutherford. He wrote to Bowman about a new house which he had built; it was two stories high and cost sixteen hundred dollars to build. Quite clearly it was such a house as Lucinda had wanted. He also informed Bowman of his intention to remarry. His second marriage was to Harriet Hutcherson, of Springfield, Illinois, whom he had met during the *Matson* trial. That was the last letter. John Bowman, perhaps unhappy about Dr. Rutherford's intentions to marry again, must have, as a gesture of severe disapproval, returned the letters of Hiram and Lucinda. These letters have been carefully kept by Dr. Rutherford's descendants, and are here, for the first time, published in their entirety.

The Letters

1. *Letter of Dr. Hiram Rutherford to John Bowman, March 10, 1841. Independence.*

Dear Sir

It gives me much satisfaction to be enabled to address you from my new home, from the far West the land of Praries & the vine.

I shall say but little of my adventures since I left Lykens Valley. Suffice it to say that without accident or incident of any particular interest I arrived in Illenois in Dec. last. I was about two weeks in selecting a location which I have done; for so far much to my satisfaction. The price of medical services is about double what it is in your country & the range of practice is about as large as the upper end of Dauphin county.[1] I have been kept busy ever since I located without loosing a single patient. I already feel my footing to be firm. I have had some seven cases of scarlet fever which is a new complaint here, & my success & knowledge of the disease has been much to my advantage. In some sections if a child gets a bad cold with sore throat the Demon (Scarlet fever) arises in the minds of the parents; & the new Doctor—booted & spurred has to dance attendance forthwith. From the frequent vicissitudes of temperature & the level, flat, & in general wet country more sickness prevails than in the East but disease is much more mild & susceptible of successful treatment. I beleive that much of the ill health is owing to bad accommodations, and carelessness of the patients themselves. It is thought that sickness diminishes much in proportion to the improvement of the country, which is rapidly advancing.

But you will be expecting something on the subject of trade. Merchandise rates at about double the price it is with you. Groceries at about 1/3d higher. Much is done on the credit system but people settle evry Christmas and give notes or mortgages or money if they have it. Merchandise of the coarsest kinds sell

1. Dr. Rutherford's Pennsylvania account books have not survived, and his standard fees when he was in practice in Millersburg cannot now be ascertained. There was strong competition in Pennsylvania, however, and in Independence, an area where doctors were scarce, Dr. Rutherford could undoubtedly charge more.

best. Groceries can be sold always for cash. There are no stores in this place at present; last summer there was two. They united & took hogs & corn from many of their customers which pork they drove when fat to the Wabash river and sold for cash. They sold last year 15 thousand dollars worth of goods at pretty much cent per cent. Having been in buissness here several years they concluded to remove 16 miles south to the county town to settle their dues & next summer there will not be more than one store for a country extending N & South 35 miles & six broad (average) extending along the Embarras River. Every season fresh settlers come pouring in & next summer large numbers are coming in. The soil is as rich as any you ever saw & produces by the most careless farming abundant crops. This country is situated about 40 miles west of the Wabash river which is our great outlet for produce.[2] A thrifty farmer can make more money here by stock produce etc than he can in the state of Ohio. The price of a first rate farm is about 8 dol per acres. Still many good ones can be obtained at Congress price[3] if a man would chose to settle a ½ mile out in the prarie. Prarie land is the best; it produces better than timber land and resists the draught better than any other kind of soil.[4] Good prarie land can be cropped in corn 10 or 15 years without impairing its fertility: the soil at an average is 18 inches deep. The first settlements made here was about 9 years ago, at that time the country was inhabited by Indians.

One of the stores has attached to it a comfortable dwelling house & stable; it could be rented for 100. dol per year. Or there are lots which a man could have from 20 to 45 dollars on which he might build with comparitively little cost. I will not be so bold as to positively advise you to come out but I should be sorry for my part to go back. There are two or three reasons why I should

2. Goods were sent down the Wabash to Terre Haute, but transportation to the Wabash, especially in rainy weather, was a major problem, for the roads became virtually impassable.

3. Land in the public domain sold for $1.25 an acre.

4. Early settlers in the area (especially Southerners) tended to avoid prairie land and to clear the trees from the land near streams for their fields. The prairie sod was initially difficult to prepare for farming.

wish you to come out which I will not at present name & shall only do so in that event. One great difference will be observed between the East & the West—that whilst the former remains in Status quo, as the Lawyers term it, the latter is marching on with giant strides. Money is perhaps scarcer here than with you; it brings 12 per cent interest.[5] If you should determine to set your face to the West, let me know of it, as I may be able to furnish you with some useful advice & information. At all events write & let me know how you are & also how the Millersburg branch of your family is & where they all are & where they may likely be in the ensuing summer.

H. Rutherford

Direct to Oakland P.O. Coles Co. Illenois

N B Tell me if Hutchinsons are still at Goods Mill & if not where they are. The price of produce here rates as follows wheat 50 cts, corn 20, oats 20, pork 3 cts per pound.[6] There are great numbers of deer here—as well as all other sorts of game. A Venison Saddle[7] of the best kind can be had for 75 cts.

P.S. Write & tell me the news from Millersburg. Remember me to Col Salladar, your wife, Josiah & Levi, your mother and Lucinda.[8] Tell me if the latter has yet returned from Philad.[9]

H. R.

5. Money was indeed scarce in Illinois. In the summer of 1841, the state government could no longer pay interest on bonds, and Illinois was at that time often called a "ruined state." For an excellent account see "Wreck of the Internal Improvement System" in Theodore Calvin Pease, *The Frontier State, 1818–1848*, pp. 216–35.

6. These prices are consistent with commodity goods prices in Chicago. See "Commodity Prices 1840–1860, Chicago." (available through University of Illinois Library).

7. A large venison roast.

8. Millersburg was approximately fifteen miles north of Harrisburg. We are unable to identify several of the acquaintances of Dr. Rutherford in Lykens Valley. Although Dr. Rutherford had reservations about many of the people he had known around Millersburg, he seems to have made several friends and often inquired of them in his letters.

9. Lucinda Bowman had been visiting her sister in Philadelphia during the winter of 1840–41.

The Letters

2. Letter of Dr. Hiram Rutherford to John Bowman, July 14, 1841.
Independence.

Dear Sir

Your letter arrived here in due course of mail. I can assure you that your letter gave me no small satisfaction. Your news of Millersburg & vicinity was news to me. Of that place I shall speak but breifly. I spent two & ½ years in that place, either to my proffit or not is not the question but be my trials as they were. I do cherrish & ever will cherrish a fond rememberance of that Locality. It is probable there are but few places in the world which are blessed with as large a number of full blood Scandalizers[1] as Millersburg yet few possess in my estimation a few choice objects as choice as a verry few in that town.[2] My thoughts recur almost evry day to old Pennsylvania.

I am glad to find you appreciate the merits of the Governor of Penn. I receive a Harrisburg paper and I find that he is equaly as bad as Matty Van was if not worse. His conduct towards the last legislature was most diabolical. The Revenue Bill which finally passed was an honor to the State.[3]

You state the Spring was late &c. It was the same here. Oats is short but other grain is good. Corn notwithstanding the dryness of the season is good. This is owing to our level country and the power prairie land has above all others of resisting drouth. I am much grattified to learn you have raised a son. An Old Veteran once told me that making boys was like running bullets—that

1. Scandalmongers.

2. Lucinda Bowman was, to Dr. Rutherford, one of the "choice objects" of Millersburg.

3. Dr. Rutherford was a Whig, and his political biases are evident in his comments on Pennsylvania Governor David Porter and President Martin Van Buren, both Democrats. In 1841 Pennsylvania had no money in the treasury to pay interest on bonds. In April of that year, the legislature passed an act "whereby banks were required to furnish immediately to the treasury a sum of $3,100,000, and were authorized to issue, in proportion to their capital and in addition to their regular circulation, relief notes secured by the pledge of the state." Governor Porter vetoed the bill, knowing it would pass over his veto. After two years of stringent economies, the state was again able to pay interest on its bonds. Wayland F. Dunaway, *A History of Pennsylvania*, pp. 391–92.

the excess material made the handle of the cast & vica versa. This simple way of reasoning I wish you to remember and put in practice. I mean to state this fact to a sister of mine who has had 3 girls in repeat for her especial benefit.

Of the people round about you I can form an opinion of from your eloquent description and my personal knowledge of them. It is in fact living a terrible life in their midst. I was glad to escape from Lykens Va[lley]. I believe if I had remained there in the course of time I should have been far distant from the way in which I was brought up. It was a great inducement for me to leave the diggins that I might break some ruinous habits which I was contracting. Here I am the same man I ever was except my vices & them I hope never to resume.

I shall now proceed to the object of this letter viz to advise you to come to Illenois. There is at this time no merchant in this place and I know not when there will be one. There is but little merchandise in all the country; the pressure of the times have prevented merchants from raising supplies and any kind of goods will sell. If you would bring on you old peices & coarse stuffs you could soon dispose of them. Groceries always bring cash and are to be had in Cincinnatti or St Louis. A store is wanted badly, people have to go 25 miles & then not get what they want perhaps. The man who has just quit has done so to collect. He has made in 3 or 4 years from nothing to several thousand dollars. This is a great grazing country & has many rich land holders. The pork trade is still pretty good. It is the custom to settle all accounts at Christmas. Debts are more easily collected by law than in P. The law is much better.[4] A stand can be had on verry reasonable terms. It is to be hoped that times will improve. I feel evry confidence in the new administration[5] and I beleive the same feeling is general throughout the country. It is hoped that the late reighn of misrule may never be repeated. By all means get out of that black hole you now live

4. It is not clear why Dr. Rutherford thought debts were more easily collected in Illinois than in Pennsylvania.

5. John Tyler, Whig, had succeeded to the presidency following the death of William Henry Harrison, Whig.

in. It is enough to kill the devil and the idea of remaining to me would be horrifying.

It is not to be supposed that when a man is leaving one place for another that he is leaving Gommorrough for a land of milk & honey. Evry one must be prepared for disappointments, but if in the aggregate he can better himself it is his duty to do it. For my own sake I could wish you to come. An old friend would be dear to me. I can suppose that you feel a difficulty about leaving a mother, brothers & sisters but these ties however dear cannot always be preserved. A day of separation as shure as the sun shines will arrive. You might bring them with you or at least some of them.

I am still in a state of single blessedness & will probably ever remain so unless you bring me a spare rib from Old M[illersburg]. I shall feel very much disappointed if you do not. I am still getting along in buissness with my old success. I have not yet lost a patient and have enjoyed better health than I have for the last 3 years. As to the health of this country I consider it good—diseases yield much easier to medicine than in the East. In the months of July & August fever [is] common but it is a mere trifle. A little calomel, salt petre & opium is sufficient.[6] Not 1 in 200 die of it. Those who have it contract it by carelessness—

---

6. It is not clear which fever Dr. Rutherford was treating with "a little calomel, salt petre & opium." As Phyllis A. Richmond noted in "Glossary of Historical Fever Terminology" in *Theory and Practice in American Medicine*, pp. 105–6, "a recurring problem for the medical historian is that of correlating the old names for diseases with modern disease entities." Richmond observed that multiple definitions reflect confusion in disease differentiation. We give here a few examples from her glossary.

Ague	malaria
Bilious Fever	typhoid; malaria
Bilious Remittent Fever	malaria; undulant fever
Bloody Flux	dysentery
Intermittent Fever	malaria
Malignant Bilious Fever	yellow fever
Putrid Fever	typhus
Remittent Fever	malaria
Sore Throat Distemper	diphtheria

open houses and wild fruit. If you should conclude to come let me know of it in time for me to get you [to] bring me a lot of medicines of which I will send you a bill to be got of D W Gross, Harrisburg.

Remember me to your family and those in M. Also to the Hutchisons. Please write soon & give me some more news.

Yours Respectfully
H. Rutherford

P.S. I am astonished to find S Alleman[7] again in M. tell me how the medical faculty progress & also whether the absent member returned with you from P. She is no doubt a dear sister to you but no one in this world occupies more of my thoughts. Remember me to her (confidential). I shall expect to hear from you soon.

H. R.

3. *Letter of Dr. Hiram Rutherford to John Bowman, October 28, 1841. Independence.*

Dear Sir

Yours of the 9th of Sept. as well as a previous letter, came to hand since I last wrote to you. I assume my pen with a variety of feelings and motives which it would be difficult to describe on paper. On you I cheifly depend for news from Lykens valley & Millersburg in particular You have told me much, but you have left in doubt & silence much that I wished to know. Of your own family in M. you tell nothing satisfactory. Your words would seem to imply that they are in trouble—from sickness or what else is left to conjecture. Tell me more of them. I feel a deep solicitude for their welfare. You say Josiah has moved back into that dark corner of Lykens. I am astonished that he, after giving his boys a good education, should bring them into association with the bipeds of that Botean locality.[1]

7. Unidentified
1. Josiah was John Bowman's brother. A boeotian is a dull, obtuse person.

I approve much of your resolution to visit the West. If you do, you will never regret it. The change of scenery from those rocky mountains & rolling valleys of Penn. to first, the deep forests, & then the level wide spread praries of Illenois, with their coats of green, their deep rich soil & their multitudinous sweet smelling flowers would give verse to a post. You say you often picture to your mind my erattic professional course, as I ride from house to house, now slow, & again on the <u>lope</u> as I leave for another point where my services are required. Your indulgence in such reveries is a high compliment to the estimate you must have of myself. But suffer me a moment to describe the reality as near as I can. My first care of a summer morning is to feed my horses. After breakfast I mount & take the road; having escaped the timber, I strike into the prarie & steer for a distant arm of the river well wooded for miles; into this forest I plunge & after doing my buissness on its near side, I take across to the other, & again emerge on an endless expanse of green: here the tools of the art are again employed, & again I mount for some far distant point. In the afternoon a different direction is persued and as night sees me again at home, & claims repose after the fatigues of the day: I draw bridle for a new day and the exertions under another sun is contemplated for future hours. But ere my foot is out of the stirrup, here comes a man at full gallop with his coat of Jean fluttering in the evening breeze. Some one is bad. I must go with all haste, and soon the forest echoes with the rappid footfalls of our high mettled horses.

The practice of medicine here is not what it is in Millersburg. I can picture to myself the deportment of the Doctors there. The anxiety & joy each feels over each patient they get, and the deep malice they feel for one another—and all this for a <u>living</u>. I can assure you I often shudder when I think of what I underwent in M. No consideration could ever draw me back to practice medicine there; to bear the insolence of some purse proud fool, or the tittle tattle of the old women and the suspicious regard of the young men, is more than I ever wish to be burthened by again. Here I walk a lord of the soil. The Doctor is the greatest man in the country, and though however ample the means of the merchant, the farmer, or the grazier, it is their interest to acquire the good will of the physician. This state of things is pleasant and though no feeling of dogmatism is in me yet it is pleasant to do good & see a community grateful for the benefits. Here is none of the tittle tattle: the low mean malice of the envious nor the loud dogmatism of the powerful. You know M. perhaps better than me; & you know one thing, that the more useful the man, and the more prosperous his affairs, the greater and bitterer his enemies will be. I do not claim for the people here an immunity from the evil natures of men, but I beleive there is a great difference in different communities. I have been taken by the hand here and have now the professional buissness of nearly the whole country.

You speak of health, of your fears of a sickly country. Health in Illenois has this season been good. In this section of the country, however it has been about the same as other years. It began about mid July and ended about the middle of this month—duration, 3 months. The principal complaint was remittant & billious fever; mostly remittant however. I had a few difficult cases but the common run was easily cured. Generally it was not necessary to visit a patient more than once or twice. I was confined to bed 4 or 5 days with the fever in Sept but have since that been quite well and able to pursue my buissness. I lost no patients no way—none died nor none left me for anybody else. Indeed I have lost but one patient since I have been in the country & that was a child which died of Thrush.[2] I am enabled to persue a much better and bolder practice here than in M. The people here call in time & take medicine as it is prescribed. There is no clique of old Dutch women over the patient, laying the medicine aside and <u>brouching</u> instead.[3] Sickness here attacks those mostly who live on coarse food and in open houses: those who live comfortably are seldom sick. I beleive that in 20

2. Thrush is a disease found especially among children. It is a yeast infection and is characterized by white lesions on the membranes of the throat, lips, and mouth. The infection may become systemic and life-threatening.

3. Unidentified. The context indicates that the Pennsylvania Dutch women used their own remedies (mustard plasters on the chest, *bruscht*) instead of the medicines prescribed by the physician. *Brouching* is not listed in Marcus B. Lambert, *A Dictionary of Non-English Words of the Pennsylvania-German Dialect*.

or 30 years this will be the most healthy country in the West. My practice in July, Sept and Oct. amounts to about $150 per month. August rates at $227. For the remainder of the year it will be small. Next year I expect to sweep the board. I have now nearly all the good families in the country. Excuse me for this tedious exposure of my own affairs. I have little else to write about and therefore am priveledged to be garulous.

When you come here come in the summer, when all nature is in bloom; you will then see the green West—our luxuriant forrest land; and if you are not improved by the trip, both in body and mind, I am no prophet. Your present location in Tartarrus,[4] cooped up by mountains and poor land, is enough to make any man sick. The land of Lykens valley in this country would be called barren; nobody would pretend to till it. The roads are prime in summer, fall & winter but in the spring they are dreadful.

I perceive Pennsylvania is completely Tylerized;[5] the news reached me in 9 days after the election. Had the election in Illenois taken place after the veto not one Whig would have been returned to Congress. As it is we have 2 out of 3. There is a general cry here for a U.S. Bank.[6] The utility of such an institution in the West is incalculable. Money is scarce. Crops are good and but little market for them. Many farmers haul their wheat 180 miles to the lakes where it is $1 per bushel.

Remember me to all enquiring friends & write soon

Yours Respt.
H. Rutherford

N.B. I was not aware that you did not receive my letters free. I shall endeavor to rectify the error this time. I am glad you hold

4. Hell.
5. Controlled by Whigs pledged to Tyler.
6. The two Whigs elected to the House of Representatives in 1841 were Zadok Casey and John T. Stuart. John Reynolds, Democrat, was also elected. Dr. Rutherford obviously thought that a U.S. Bank would help end the economic crisis in the West and stabilize the monetary situation. The bank was proposed by Clay and had widespread support in Western areas.

the office.[7] Enjoy life to the best advantage where you are but do not forget to visit the West. Emigration is going on at a great rate to Iowa: immense numbers pass through this place rolling on to the Far West.

H. R.

4. *Letter of Dr. Hiram Rutherford to John Bowman, April 27, 1842. Independence.*

Dear Sir,

It has been with the greatest impatience that I have watched the mail for the last three months for a letter from you; but none has come; and under the impression that another epistle may meet with better success in enlivening your recollections, I broach the subject once more.

You cannot conceive with what tenacity a man will cling to the objects of home, to the scenes of youthful pleasures. Every letter I receive is a perfect treat. On you I depend for my Lykens Valley correspondence. Pray do not desert me. I also wrote to your people in Millersburg as much as twice, but all there is silence to me. What is the matter? Why is it that I receive no answer—Have you deserted me and have <u>they</u> forgotten me—The thought comes like sickness over my soul. How often have I wished that I could suddenly step into your family circle and enjoy your surprize. But dear me a great wilderness separates me from all I love, & 18 months must elapse as the nearest period at which I may see the dearest jewels of my heart.

You may infer from this language that I am discontented with my situation. But this is far from being the case. Fortune has smiled on me and she still covers me as with a mantle. I live in peace—my practice is large and I am possessed of houses and lands. When at leisure I read, sleep, think or smoke my cob-

7. The address on the envelope indicates Bowman had become postmaster of Elizabethville, Pennsylvania. The recipient at that time normally paid the postal fee, and Dr. Rutherford must have assumed that Bowman, as postmaster, would be exempt. It was possible for the sender to pay the postage, and Dr. Rutherford seemed to indicate that he would, in the future, follow that practice.

pipe—recline in my chair with my feet elevated upon the table and puff, puff as the smoke of the consuming tobacco ascends above & in slow gyrations is disolved in the atmosphere arround. But 'all is not gold that glitters'—this is my favorite occupation when thoughts of other scenes press heavily on my soul. And the semblance of outward composure is but too often in an inverse ratio to the strife within. Conscience makes cowards of us all, and necessity—the robbers plea—is invoked to calm the rising sperit. When I left for the West I knew not when I should return. If fortune was not kinder in the land of strangers than in that of friends, I knew not when I might revisit familiar scenes. I left home poor. When I came to the West I resolved to turn over a new leaf, to forego follies & take a broader base of action. I have lived almost like a hermit in my private capacity, standing aloof from local broils etc and bending my whole attention to the legitimate purposes of my profession. The result so far is favourable and I hope in time to return an independent man, and putting to rights some <u>things</u> which I should never have left wrong—so conscience says.

I would again urge upon you a visit to Illenois, not only for the benefit of your health but for the enjoyment of the journey. The roads are now first rate[1] & the eye will never tire of the flowers of the wilderness and of the prarie: and the scent of their blooms and the brightness of their colors is unsurpassed by Moores 'Vale of Cashmere'[2] whilst at the same time the eye can view mile upon mile and still rest upon an endless expanse of green. Come now whilst nature is fresh and see the virgin productions of this alluvial soil.

Times here are hard; money is scarce, & what is to be had is of but little account. A most overpowering pressure sits upon the land. Property is extremely cheap.[3] I myself however am able to stand above the storm. Prudence and echonemy are recquisite now in a most eminent degree. From what I can learn

1. Most certainly an exaggeration, for most of the roads had not been greatly improved by 1842.

2. Dr. Rutherford is referring to *Lalla Rookh* (1817) by Thomas Moore (1779–1852).

3. Following the Panic of 1837, the economy of Illinois was still depressed.

the pressure is not confined to the West, but the East also has its portion.

A drove of Buffaloes passed through here toward the East lately.[4] These animals are quite a curiosity. They resemble our cattle of the Durham breed more than any other tame animals. The fore parts are much higher than the hind & heavier. They run with great swiftness—make a grunting noise & have a beard like a goats. With the drove (33 in number) was a female Elk. It is two or 3 times the size of a deer & in the wild state must possess great swiftness.

The winter has been uncommonly mild, in consequence considerable sickness has prevailed—mostly pleurisies & diseases of the lungs. I have been well myself except for 2 or 3 months I was troubled with a diarrhea which was kept up by constant riding and exposure to the chilly blasts of the prarie.

The currency is terribly deranged, a man is not safe at present in any kind of Bank paper.[5] Specie is no more to be seen; it is amongst the things that were.

A man could do a good buissness here store keeping. I own a house & storeroom which I should just like to let you into. Do leave that Stygian vale. Necessity kept me there and necessity drove me away—to stay I could but creep—to go I knew I could walk. If I return it will be but for a short season and though I hope to see the day when old Dauphin will be more prosperous than at present, yet in Lykens Valley but few bright spots illumines the pleasures of memory—for my old stomping ground the ties of kindred are sufficient to hallow its holy precincts.

Remember me to your family—to those in Millersburg my best wishes for their welfare. If you should conclude to take a pleasure trip hence advise me when I may expect you. But above all things do not neglect to answer this letter & tell me all concerning yourself & every body else. If you dont, I shall feel extremely unhappy.

Yours
H. Rutherford

4. This is a late sighting of buffalo in Illinois.

5. Paper money was heavily discounted and deeply distrusted in Illinois in 1842, and specie (coins) had virtually disappeared, as Dr. Rutherford remarked.

The Letters

5. Letter of John Bowman to Dr. Hiram Rutherford, May 13, 1842. Elizabethville, Pa.

Dear Sir

Yours of Aprile 27th was received as also your former letter. I can assure you it is gratifying to me to hear from an olde acquaintance. But the only apoligy I can justly make as to the delay in not answering yours is carelessness. I suppose I thought as often as fifty times about writing to you but some how never got at it. I will endeavor for the future to make amends for all former slothfullness. In the first place I will just say I am reasonably well at this time. But have been this spring greatly troubled with a pain in the head and at times uncommonly weak. I sometimes think that that old complaint of the liver is still lurking within. Though I feel no pain in the side, which is said to be the greatest symptoms of liver complaints. Our family at old Millersburg are all well at this time, also my own family. Our country has been healthy: notwithstanding that some have died that you were acquainted with. Joseph Sallade was buried on the 20th of last month. Times are Tuff here, oweing to the currency derangement. Country Banks are at a discount in Phil. from 10 to 15 pct. Releif notes 20, which makes business poor, particularly here, as we have none other but country Bank paper amongst us. I have often wished myself away from here. But these times the less business you do the better, unless it were a cash business. As soon as a prospect of better times illumines the Atmosphere, and I live and keep health, my name will be <u>Haines</u>[1] and if I should not get further than to Millersburg again, still better than this section of country for business. Josiah has left Millersburg & Henry Shammer of Halifax occupies his rooms with a store. Doct. Rathbon lives in his house opposite mothers. Old Rathbon & the Doct. had a fall out. Millersburg does not improve much. [Illegible word] feeder still unfinished

1. Possibly a reference to Daniel Haines (1801–1877), who was elected governor of New Jersey in 1843. He was a participant in the "Broad Seal War" of 1839. Five Whigs elected to the New Jersey legislature had their seats contested, even though they had "certificates of election under the broad seal of the State." The Democrats were seated.

and nothing doing at it and probably now never will be finished unless the Legislature gives it to a Company. There was some talk of that last winter. John Frederick has solde out to D. Welker. Frederick has gone to the City of Phila. and in company with several others, commenced a business in the whole sale way. his family is still in Millersburg. But I believe intends moving them down also in the falle.

Welker cuts a large swath in olde Millersburg when he gets his wet sheet aboarde. he makes some fine propositions to the young bucks, that want wives. any young fellow he will bellow out in the store, That marries one of my daughters, can step right in a fine chance for speculation. Olde Gen'l. Seal is still dealing out grog. Burch and Allaman are still teaching school there. There is nothing new strange or uncommon about & about what it was when you left, marriages are few and far between; though some are still venturing into it. Lights daughter was married a short time ago. We have had quite an open Winter & Spring Colde thus far, now getting something warmer. Though night frosts occassionally happen yet Fruit not injured much yet. grain this spring looks well, wheat is selling here at $1.15. Rye 75. I should like uncommonly well to visit you in the State of Illenoise, but I dont think I can just now: The times here are completely out of joint and it will be no small time I fear, before the prospect of better times, brightens the drooping spirit of Penna. As to myself, I think I can get along without the aid of a Surgeon; Our country at this time is completely drained of money. Banks do not discount, and what money is in the country is gotten up by those that have payments to make in the Banks: But hope the last refuge of man comes on apace; and distorts the glimmerings of a change of times: amidst the phantoms of Imaginations: We may revel awhile in castles built in the air; But the christians hope, will do more when well grounded: he can soar beyond the Empyreal <u>Sphere</u>, and with eyes intellectual, veiw the first good, first perfect, & first <u>fair</u>, and when this earth be rolled up as a parchment scroll, The Christians hope will leade him <u>there</u>. The which thought is a source of consolation and tends to meloirate all connected with sublunary things. Benjaman Kepner & Samuel Faune is out for Sheriff. Doct. Rathbon for prothonotary.[2] Faune still lives in Millersburg and at this time is out of business of any kinde. He keeps an open house Liquor Free. it is a fine watering place for some of them Millersburg chaps, as long as it lasts.

!Hypothetical!!

You mentioned that you hade written to our family at Millers-burg, ande receivede no answer. Of that I am ignorant ande dide not know that you hade written to any member of the family there. Why they dide not answer you I cannot tell. If to my Sister Lucinda you wrote, which is only conjecture by me: I can probably guess at it why you received no answer. Delicacy or timidity was doubtless the cause. She is a quiet [illegible] person; and [illegible] sister. I love her. She has a minde as deep as the Salt mines of Polands, and can preserve: anything confidede to her: equally with that mineral. That probably accounts why I dide not get to finde out that you hade wrote. ....

!!Conscience!! Connected with human nature the close ob-server, may discover that high sense of honor which aught in reality be the Appindages of every man. But to err is human, nothing short of the finer feelings of the Soul, in a highly Cul-tivated minde can feel the deep poignancy of Conscience—: Your [letter] contains so many things. That I am really at a loss to answer all: Should you discover anything on this page that you do not understand, pray do not construe it in any way more nor less than good will, goode humour, and my best wishes for your success.—When a man writes upon a subject he does not understand, he must ask the person addressed to excuse and pardon all imperfections in his composition: I therefore aske it of you in this.

Write to me soon again, and I will again write to you, and give you all the news—&c. You mentioned that you hade a house with store room attached that would just suit: I could put in my stock, and you the house &c, and go halfs, if times were not so miserable bade, if so be we were inclined that way. But more of

2. A chief clerk in a court of law.

this at another time. Write soon and let me know how times &c move along among the wilds of that Western clime.

I am With Respect your
OBE Svrt
<u>John</u> J <u>Bowman</u>

6. *Letter of Dr. Hiram Rutherford to John Bowman, July 31, 1842.*
Independence.

Dear Friend

I feel myself most happy for your favor of May last. I had almost despaired of ever receiving farther intelligence from you, being well aware that the profit of the correspondence was all on my own side; whilst you had nothing to gain by soiling paper for my gratification—I could tell you nothing of particular interest in return; for, notwithstanding the mind will naturally glow, at a mental or corporeal view of this green land with all its fruits and flowers, yet without the associations of human affection, it is almost as dreary as the Solitude of Selkirk[1]—ergo having never breathed the air of the West, nor gazed upon the blue dome above, from its rolling mounds, nor having neither kindred nor friends under its starry vault, with whom the associations of love might hallow its precincts—it cannot be expected that you should feel any thing but a passive indifference to its locality. But with me the case is reversed. The East is the land of my birth—it is the home of my fathers. Amongst its rugged hills and winding streams, I have spent my early days. In close communion lives nearly all that is dear to me from the ties of blood. In one church yard is buried all my kindred, whom God has pleased to call away; and to the same enclosure, the hand of time beckons the remainder home.[2] Whether I shall lie down in that place with them, God only knows; but it has always

1. The solitary life of Alexander Selkirk (1676–1721) on an uninhabited island inspired sections of Daniel Defoe's *Robinson Crusoe* (1719).
2. Dr. Rutherford's ancestors were buried in Paxtang, Pennsylvania.

been my fervent prayer that my dust might nestle by its kindreds ashes.

Apart from home the next place which holds in my affections is Lykens Valley. I do not mean to embrace the entire region of country comprehended by that name; but allude to a few sperits which breathe in its shade. Amongst the most prized of those, permit me to name yourself. The recollections connected with your section of country, has many green spots in my memory. For this I value much your correspondence; I can assure you that no day or night passes over my head, but what the recollections of old Millersburg have a place in my thoughts. Your correspondence therefore is a great gratification to me, although I am of course incapacitated from making you a like return.

You mention your being in an invalid state. My dear fellow follow my prescription, and take a trip to the West—it would cure you as sound as a trout. I am in excellent health at present—Whether this is due to the recuperative powers of the constitution, or to the virtues of the Washingtonian temperance pledge is not material. I feel just as well as I ever did in my life.

Your hypothetical conjecture, with respect to which member of your family I had written, was correct: but I cannot agree with you as to the cause of my receiving no answer to my letters. The qualities of Delicacy and Timidity I know her to be possessed of in an exalted degree. But they would not have been wounded by writing to me, if she regarded me as she once did. We corresponded by letter before I left the East, and we parted in Philad. with a vow to write to each other, as soon as she should return to Millersburg. But now my dear friend I hope you will pardon, and look with a feeling of compassion upon me, when I make the unworthy confession, that when I solicited your correspondence, an all prominent motive was, that I might hear of her, and learn her whereabouts. I touched through delicacy, the subject lightly, but you never seemed to take the hint. I only learnt by you that she had returned. To her I then wrote, and wrote, but no answer ever came. I cannot tell you with what feelings I saw the mail arrive, week after week, and yet nothing came for me. It was then and not till then, that I ventured to be more explicit to yourself, and now immodest as it is, I have ventured to unfold my feelings to your view. But I have one consolation; I know that I can do it confidentially. I could not write to any body else, because I felt an insurmountable repugnance to exposing the secret wish of my soul to the public gaze, especially to have our connection discussed, & critizized by <u>some</u> of the bipeds of Millersburg.

I will not enter upon the reasons why Lucinda and I did not marry before I left the East—one was I was poor; but I hoped that when 3 years would have rolled over, that I could return and reclaim her; and, with becomming honor offer her a home with me in the West. I know that her sentiments have not changed with regard to me. I judge of them from what I know of her, and also from my own feelings; 'Time but the impression deeper makes,' and mine are impressed on a basis, as immutable as the iron granite of your mountains. But O John why will you not solicit her confidence on this subject. You are her favorite brother. She has often told me so, and answer, why she never wrote. I can hardly think that my letters miscarried, because none of my others have.

On looking over what I have written, I sensibly feel the delicacy of the Subject. I feel that it might look to some, like a childish complaint; and unsatisfied as I feel, in my mind of the propriety of what I have committed to paper I will yet rest on your goodness of heart, for a charitable interpretation of my motives.

I remain Yours &c.
H. Rutherford

N.B. Times are bad enough. The whole West is now groaning under the cut throat policy of Capt Tyler.[3] Wheat will not bring 25 cts a bushel at our best markets. Corn will be worth about 10 or 12 cents. I shall look for an answer soon; pray do not disappoint me & I shall ever remain your obliged &c H. Rutherford.

3. President Tyler's veto of Clay's bill to establish a national bank enraged most Whigs. Dr. Rutherford blamed Tyler for the continued depressed state of the Western economy.

The Letters

7. Letter of Dr. Hiram Rutherford to John Bowman, November 24, 1842. Independence.

Dear Sir

Excuse the delay I have made in answering your last valuable letter. Buissness has been urgent till the present time. There has been considerable sickness this fall hereabouts. Winter has come unusually soon. Several snows have fallen; but like the clouds of King Richard 'in the deep boosom of the mud lie buried'[1] at present the ground is frozen & 2 or 3 inches of snow lies upon it. We have had some cold weather; so cold indeed, that one of my ears froze in the Prairie. I have since I last wrote, enjoyed good health, but am sorry to hear that yours is but reasonable. Your news is new to me, & I appreciate it as an exile in a distant land. Oh how delightful it is to hear news from where I am bound by the tenderest ties.

There is one subject upon which you wrote however, which of course you well knew would be unsatisfactory to me. Why did you do part and leave the rest? Delicacy, yes, delicacy! So note it be. You gave Lucinda my letter & she sent it back. But forgive me, friend, I have no right to judge your feelings.—We estimate men too much perhaps from the shade of our own thoughts, and as in the fable of the Spectacles, their hue is according to the medium through which we see them. I did not expect Lucinda would travel up to Paynterstown to tell you how the case was, delicacy might forbid it; but I did expect you would say something to her on the subject, although I knew your habits and thoughts were moody and solitary, and your delicacy fastidious. But pray good friend take no offense, although your letter sadly disappointed me. Be kind enough to deliver the enclosed to her. I take the liberty of sending it to her by your hands, which liberty excuse, as I wish to be certain of her getting it. Whether she answers this last epistle or not, this will probably be the last time in our correspondence in which I shall allude to

1. William Shakespeare, *Richard III*: "And all the clouds that low'r'd upon our house/In the deep bosom of the ocean buried" (I, 1. 3–4).

[27]

the subject. However I shall take it as a high boon, if you shall continue to advise me of her health and happiness. You may ask, but if all be well, when will you return? If she should answer me according to my desires I may probably return in 3 months, but certainly in six; if she does not, I do not expect ever to be back, at least not for years yet, and then it will only be at the urgent solicitation of my aged parents.

You hoped my motives were pure. My disposition is not one to take fire from a stragling spark. Your relation to her well justifies your guardian care. I can assure you I might in my opinion connect myself with the fairest, and most wealthy of this land, if my taste did not lead me another way. You may think that I might have set all to rights before I left; as things have turned out, I might, I know; but I did not know everything. I was venturing beyond the aid of Friends—a stranger in a strange land, and naturaly timid I feared to bring any one to want from my misfortunes. I thought to return in season, and bring her to my new home, which I trust and pray I may yet be able to do.

Crops have been abundant. Corn, wheat &c in profusion, prices low & money scarce.

A specimen of Illenois pumpkins is to [be] seen at Springfield. One weighs 224 pounds.[2] In future I shall promise you more details of this country than at present; please write soon and oblige your friend.

H. Rutherford

8. *Letter of Lucinda Rutherford to Mrs. Frances Bowman, [June] 26, 1843. Independence.*

Dear Mother

I now take my pen in hand to address you. We arrived here on the last day of May after a tedious and fatigueing journey; I intended writing immediately after we arrived, but have been

2. Dr. Rutherford probably read about the pumpkin in Illinois newspapers. Accounts of large fruits and vegetables were often published in the newspapers of that time. Dr. Rutherford is using the fertility of the land in his continued efforts to convince the Bowmans to emigrate to Illinois.

prevented from one cause or another, untill the present. I shall first attempt to give you a history of our toilsome journey to the west, I commence at Millersburg the day we left that we traveled 26 miles, staid in Mifflintown, the next day we traveled about 40 miles, staid in a small town called Millscrick, and the day after that which was friday we arrived in Hollydaysburg about 3 O clock in the afternoon, we staid with a cousin of the Dr the name of Calvin, from there we pushed on untill we arrived in Pittsburg, we staid there a day as Dr had some business there, from thence we traveled on untill we arrived in ohio amongst our friends, remained there 8 days, the time passed by pleasantly, visiting amongst the friends, I was very much pleased with the country and the people, we left there on tuesday the 23 of May and arrived in Indianopolis on friday following, we staid there untill Monday, staid at an acquaintanse of the Dr from Harrisburg, Indianopolis is a very handsome place, not quite as large as Harrisburg but fully as handsome I think, we left there on monday and pushed on untill we arrived at Independence Ills my new home, I am very well pleased with the country and tolerably with the town we reside in.[1] It is very small hardly as large as Painterstown, but there is one consolation, there is no talebearing nor scandalizers, a person can live in peace, and you never hear anything but English, I have not heard a word of german since I have been here, althoug there are some germans settled around. The society is poor here, still the folks are very clever quite different from what they are in the east, several called to see me the day we arrived and wellcomed me to Pin Hook a nick name they have given the town.[2]

The praries here are delightful, they are from 12 to 20 miles wide, and 150 long, instead of the timber surrounding them, they surround the timber, at this season they are most beautiful,

1. Lucinda's estimates of distances seem to be generally accurate. The names of the friends and relatives visited along the way cannot be determined now. Indianapolis, settled in 1820, was a thriving small city in 1843. It had begun to develop rapidly after it became the state capital, and its growth was enhanced with the coming of the National Road.

2. A *pinhook* was a fishing hook made from a pin. See Dr. Rutherford's comments on the name "Pin Hook" in pt. 2, art. 3.

The green grass has sprung up and covered the whole bosom of these wastes; with that grass there springs up a multitude of flowers of every hue, form, and scent, It is delightful to ride over this level land and every step, tramping those gems of nature underfoot. Their beutiful heads can be seen as far as the eye can reach waving in the summer wind. I think when we get to housekeeping I shall be delighted with this country, we have not got to housekeeping yet in consequence of not having our goods yet. As we passed through Terre-Haute[3] comeing out we stopped and inquired about our boxes but were informed that they had not arrived yet, they had no boats come up the river for two weeks on account of the wabash river not being navigable, the Dr received a letter a few days agoe from Terre Haute and was informed that they had not arrived but that the wabash was in a faire navigable order at that time, he said he had understood that there was a great many goods stored at Evansville Indiana from different places, yet to come up the wabash and several boats looked for to come with goods, ours probable will be amongst them. The distance from here to Terre-Haute is 40 miles on the other side of the Wabash river from here, I hope we will get them, if we do not I expect to be as poor as holly shanks garden.[4] I am almost tired boarding, though the people we board with are very clever and accommodating, I feel perfectly at home. The house we are going too live is but one story high, there is 3 rooms and a kitchen, quite a neat little house, the houses here are all only one story, principally log cabins in the country, The Dr has gone this day to Paris 18 miles from here the nearest stoers to get what things we need yet towards housekeeping. there are a great quantity of strawberrys here the largest and best I ever eat,[5] I go out very frequently and gather them, ride horse-back, I preserve some, they are very nice, we

3. Terre Haute, Indiana, was strategically located on the Wabash. Produce from the Oakland area could be taken to Terre Haute and then loaded on steamboats. Goods shipped to Oakland by way of Terre Haute were unloaded from boats in Terre Haute and sent the rest of the way by wagon.

4. We were unable to identify "holly shanks garden." Perhaps it is a local proverb.

5. Wild strawberries were common in that area.

have honey every meal the best kind and lots of cheese, venison, and every [thing] that is good. The provisions we took from Millersburg lasted till we got to Ohio, there we got a fresh supply which lasted out. we traveled at the rate of 15 hours every day and 18 days traveling. I am well, and enjoyed very good health since I left M. the dr is also in good health.

I feel anxious to see you all and like if some of you could come out here too see [us] I should be delighted and I know you would be pleased Doctor joins me in love to you all.

Give my love to Johns family and Josiahs, Uncel Crosson and tell cousin Mary that I intend writing too her as soon as I get to housekeeping, Give my love to all inquiring friends

from you affect daughter
L Rutherford

Write soon and let me know how matters and things are going on in the east and at home, let me know whether emma has returned from the city.

9. *Letter of Dr. Hiram Rutherford to John Bowman, October 21, 1843. Independence.*

Dear Sir

Yours of Sept 4th came to hand in due time. The news therein contained, interested us much. Every peice of news rec'd from Lykens, has its peculiar interest for us, and this letter would probably have a much more lively one in your mind, if it came from Lucinda, than as it is from me. I have been urging her for 2 weeks to the work, but she still pleads want of time and as you requested a speedy answer this epistle must suffice, till she can write to you herself.

We did not begin housekeeping till the beginning of July; and as our Boxes had not come to hand, we had as the old saying is, to shift like new beginners. We passed the warm months of July & August on a straw bed, with borrowed clothes, pretty comfortably.[1] Our cooking utensils were few indeed, but provisions, fortunately, were in abundance. During this time it appeared as if we were never to hear more of our Boxes. I wrote to the towns on the Wabash, & Evansville on the Ohio, to no effect. At last I wrote to Pittsburgh & there they were, safe enough. They were immediately sent down the river to Evansville, where I sent a waggon & team for them (distance 145 miles). We finaly recd them on the 9th of Sept. Everything was safe, nothing was broken or spoiled, even Mrs Wises bag of Snitz was in perfect preservation.[2] While I am writing the stove is full blast, and our Archer Lamp throws its brilliant light over the paper.[3] We have now 2 feather beds up, with every thing else necessary for living, & nearly every thing we <u>want</u>. The necessity for keeping up <u>caste</u> in this country is but slight: but few peoples, however wealthy, furnish their homes with anything they can do without. We had a boy 10 or 12 years old for a couple of months, when he left us. We did not find that his assistance lessend Lucinda's daily duties, & since his exit we have declined receiving any other in his stead. We find that the trouble of overseeing an eye servant, is equal to the performance of his work.[4]

Sickness has been pretty abundant. I have never done so much in one summer before, & yet I have lost but 2 patients in all my practice since my return. In August I booked about $250.[5] I have had good health. Lucinda has had several shakes of the ague, and in August while attending a camp meeting she took cold, and had the fever for two or 3 days, most reverendly.[6]

1. Straw-filled mattresses were cooler than feather mattresses and were commonly used in the summer.

2. *Schnitz* were cut up and dried apples.

3. The Rutherfords had undoubtedly acquired a solar lamp manufactured by Archer, Warner, Miskey & Co. in Pennsylvania; see Loris S. Russell, *A Heritage of Light*, p. 123. For detailed information about solar lamps, see Joseph T. Butler, *American Antiques, 1800–1900*, pp. 125–39.

4. An *eye servant* was one who had to be watched carefully.

5. Dr. Rutherford kept careful accounts of the bills owed him for his medical services. Even though he wrote $250 in his account book in August, he would have received almost no cash. He commonly accepted goods and services for many of his bills.

6. There was then no Methodist church in Independence, and Methodists in this area camped out for several days to hear sermons from a circuit preacher.

You may wish to know how she is satisfied with Illenois. As to that, she will probably speak for herself, when she writes; but I flatter myself, that she is nearly as well contented, as I am with the West. We want for but little, except the friends we left behind.

We recd a letter from Mary Jackson a few days after yours came to hand.[7]

Vegetation has been abundant. I never saw the prairies present so gorgeous an appearance as they have the past summer. They are now on fire, & the sky in all points of the horizon, is illumin'd by the glare of their fires. Wheat failed this year, corn & oats were good. Our nearest market is Layfeette, Indiana, about 80 miles distance.[8] In 2 years it will be less than 40 from us. Wheat there is worth 66, corn 28. Salt $1.60 per barrel. Coffee here is worth 12 ½ per lb. Sugar 8 ⅓. Starch 6 ¼. Tow Linnen 10 cts per yard. Dry goods are much cheaper than a few years since, [and] are all sold for cash. Our currency [is nearly] all specie, but little paper is seen. [What paper] is current is held by the merchants, [word missing] to specie. In conclusion, we live in the best house in the place, have the best water, and the best horses & cows in these diggins. Remember us to your own family, Levi, Josiah, Mother, Emeline, &c.

Please write to us soon again: & I'll engage that Lucinda will answer your next. We are in good sperits, cheer up yourself, and conceive the Boetia you live in, a verry Athens itself. The pleasures of the Imagination are unlimited.

H. Rutherford

10. *Letter of Lucinda Rutherford to Mrs. Frances Bowman, January 15, 1844. Independence.*

Dear Mother & sister

You have no doubt been looking for an answer to your very interesting letter of October 19th long ere this, I attempted sev-

---

7. Mary Jackson was Lucinda's sister. The letter has not survived.

8. Just why commodities were being sent to Lafayette, Indiana, instead of the more accessible Terre Haute, Indiana, is not clear.

eral times to answer it, but never untill the present moment, has it been accomplished, you must not think that I have forgotten you, because I have not written more frequently, No, Dear, Mother & sister I assure that my affection for you has not in the least abated, it has increased, I think of you every day of my life, and often dream of you at night, I am getting very anxious to see you, but I expect it will be several years yet before we can visit you, I have sett a time I say two years from next spring, if life and health permits us, but I hope we shall have the pleasure of haveing some of you to visit us before that time, I know you will be pleased with this country, Illenois is a delightful country to live in, Brother John talked of coming to see us next summer, he must be sure and come, Mother you or emma come with him and Margaret come, as many of you as can, I have not been much homesick yet, I am very well pleased with Illenois yet all the objection I have to the west is that it is not as healthy as the east, I had a spell of the fever last august was confined to bed 5 or six days, I have had several shakes of the ague,[1] but at present I enjoy good health and am stouter and fatter than I have been since I have been in the country. We have been keeping house since July last, I like the employment toleable well, housekeeping is attended with a great deal of care. We live in about the best house in town, though it is only one story high, 3 rooms, and a kitchen, the largest room is larger than either of your two front rooms. We have our stove in it and it makes the room quite comfortable, though the weather has been very moderate, we have two cows, I churn about 3 lb of butter every week, we have but one horse, had two but the Doctor sold one, but he intends buying another in the spring, we have six cats and any quantity of rats and mice—we had a boy a few months in the summer to assist me in doing the housework, but he has left us and since he is gone we declined getting any other in his stead, as his assistance did not lessen my daily duties any. there was consideral sickness here last summer in August, September, and October, the Doctor was scarcely a day at home, and often away all night, which made it very lonesome for me.

1. Lucinda obviously contracted malaria at the camp meeting.

The Letters

We received our boxes 9th of september, everything was safe, they had been stored up at Pittsburg.

I feel quite lost here on account of haveing meetings so seldom, ther is preaching here once a month, I beleive they dont have any prayermeetings or hall, at least I have not heard of any, the principal church is the Cumberland Presbyterian, I attended a methodist campmeeting last August, the smallest campmeeting I ever was at, there was about 12 tents, it lasted only 4 days, very poor preaching, I staid on the campground one night, I took cold there, was the cause of my having the fever, it was held 6 or 8 miles north of independence.

I have not quilted my flyer quilt yet but intend quilting it in the summer, I have not done anything on my red star quilt, I can get no red oiled calico, here, I suppose I will be obliged to leave it untill we visit Penna.[2] I have a good deal of sewing to do, two dresses, for myself to make, and several shirts for the Doctor, shams and collars, I am kept very busy, I just finished a pair of gloves for the doctor, I was 4 or 5 weeks kniting them, but you know I am a poor knitter, they are the first gloves I ever knit. we have had snow here 6 or 8 [inches] deep, it only laid a few days.

women in this country dont work as hard as they do in the east, the most of the men here milks the cows. I milk our cows myself for I despise to see a man sitting under a cow milking, I think it is a womans work. I received a letter from sister Mary some months since, I intend answering this week.[3] I received one two weeks since from cousin Mary Crosson. I read it with pleasure, she informed me of the news and changes about old Millersburg. Write soon and do not do as I did.

—later

2. The names of quilt patterns changed from locale to locale. Lucinda's *flyer* quilt has not survived, and we cannot identify the specific pattern. Her *red star* quilt is on display at the Rutherford home in Oakland. In addition to the prominent red stars, it is a friendship quilt, signed by many of Lucinda's friends before her marriage.

3. The letter from Lucinda's sister Mary is not among the Rutherford family papers.

I wrote this 3 or 4 days since, at that time was well but at present I am almost distracted with the tooth ach—I caught a cold and it settled in my teeth, my face is very much swolen I can scarcely see out one of my eyes, the Doctor is well and enjoys good health, write soon as I am anxious to hear from you, the Doctor joins me in love to you all, give my love to Unculs Crossons, Johns family, Josiah family and to all enquiring friends I am your affectionate daughter and sister

Lucinda Rutherford

11. *Letter of Dr. Hiram Rutherford to John Bowman, January 19, 1844.*

I recd your last a few days after mine departed East—and as Lucinda has at last accomplished the task of a letter I avail myself of the occasion to drop a few lines to yourself.

There has not been much sickness for the last two months. I have been engaged lately collecting money & have had better luck than common.

In consequence of a rising of the waters the mail has been detained 3 or 4 days, else our letters would have come quicker to hand. Lucinda's was written 2 or 3 days since. She has enjoyed good health all along but at present is groaning under the tooth ache—her face is much swolen. The winter has been quite open, one snow of five or 6 inches deep has fallen but soon passed away. Today is like spring. We occasionaly receive papers from you for which we are thankful. I have never been in better health and (as the most of people say when they write) hoping these few lines may find you enjoying the same blessing I bring my letter to a close awaiting an early answer

I remain yours
H. Rutherford.

12. *Letter of Dr. Hiram Rutherford to John Bowman, May 28, 1844. Oakland.*

Dear Sir
As it has chanced heretofore, that in our correspondence we

happened to both <u>think at once</u>, and our letters from a natural law of progression, necessesarily passed each other on the road, marring much the harmony of mental ink & paper exchanges— therefore having waited long for you to write <u>first</u>, and fearing that delay might cause the sperit to moove us as before, (which I can explain only by the Mesmeric principle called clairvoy- ance) I have concluded to write first myself, and should this epistle be too <u>late</u> I am determined to be beforehand with you the next time as I shall probably write again in a month or two.

In my profession there has been more than the usual quantity of buissness for this season of the year, and since I have been to the country, I have never known it so wet. I can assure you the labour of riding or rather wading through the deep mud, swim- ming the overflowing creeks, or plodding on under the soaking rain, day after day, & nights in the bargain, should entitle me to be classed with the working men notwithstanding the distinc- tions of the populare demogogues of the day.

Lucinda has enjoyed good health, except an occasional chill, which however was always light, and latterly appears to have entirely departed. However she appears to be entirely rid of that old cough she had so long. Some time ago she took cold, and to cure it took a table spoonful of Hive Syrup, instead of a teaspoonful.[1] You may imagine we had a pretty severe case on hand. She vomited nearly all day, but the remedy was effectual, the disease left directly.

We received a letter from Emeline since you wrote.[2] In it we were apprised of Mary Crosson's wedding, and besides the sur- prising news that Polly Frank was in a fair way to bestow upon her leige Lord an heir. No doubt but some peculiar race is to arise from John. Similar perhaps to Abraham of old who in his later years begat the germ of a wonderful people. I hope he will bear the precious gift with becomming meekness. However it would be well for a friend to be by with a few hoops lest some- thing dreadful might happen. A Persian Sage says it is the duty of every man, to go a journey, write a book or make a child. If

---

1. Hive syrup, containing squill, was used as an emetic and as an expectorant.
2. The letter from Emeline, Lucinda's sister, has not survived.

John had no assistance from any of his <u>good neighbors</u>, he has to heathen notions attained the cheif end of man.[3] Please give me your opinion on the subject when you write again.

June 1st

In consequence of the wretched state of the roads U.S. Mail has for the present been called off this route and I am obliged to send this letter 18 miles to get it mailed.[4] It rained every day or two and last night it poured down like the Devil.

The past winter passed over smoothly enough. Our society is tolerably good. Some young men formed a debating club and amongst other questions was one: 'Does the Scriptures teach a future enless punishment?' A day was set apart and the discussion commenced at 2.o'clock & lasted till twelve at night. There was 4 orthodox to 4 universalists. We had the fortune to beat them out and one of the Judges who was previously strong in the universal beleif renounced the doctrine on the spot. A grand discussion is to come off next week within six miles of this place between two of the greatest champions in either cause in this part of the country.

In consequence of the stoppage of the mail I have not received any papers for 2 weeks. I have rec'd a number from yourself this spring for which I must return you thanks. I would mention however that it is not necessary to send any Pa. Telegrafs[5] as I am a subscriber to it.

But little is said here on politics, Clay is the universal choice of the Whig party in this country.[6] What is your opinion of Pa. politics at next election.

3. John and Polly Frank were obviously well known to John Bowman and Dr. Rutherford. John's fathering a child at an advanced age brought forth these humorous comments from Dr. Rutherford.

4. Dr. Rutherford probably sent the letter to Paris, Illinois, to be mailed there.

5. The Pennsylvania *Telegraph*, published in Harrisburg, was a Whig newspaper.

6. An Abolitionist, Dr. Rutherford would have been known as a "Conscience Whig." Members of the proslavery segment of the party were known as "Cotton Whigs." It is worth noting that Dr. Rutherford did not comment on Clay but merely reported his popularity. Dr. Rutherford did approve of Clay's efforts to establish a U.S. Bank.

Lucinda joins me in love to you all 'hoping (as old fashioned folks say) that these few lines may find all enjoying the blessings of health equal to the Irishmans prayer "may ye niver die." '

H. Rutherford

13. *Letter of Dr. Hiram Rutherford to John Bowman, June 26, 1844. Independence.*

Yours of June 1st came to hand a few days ago. Affairs in this country look rather bad. The immense quantity of rain which has fallen has destroy[ed] in a measure our prospects. Some are still planting. The wheat has a rank appearance but from the same cause it is struck with the rust and a disease called the spot.[1] The rivers of the west are uncommonly high this season. The Wabash at this time has to be ferried nearly 2 miles. The Mississippi at St. Louis is 9 miles wide. Great destruction of property is the consequence. The month of June is generaly the best to visit this country as there is a heavy freshlet every year at that time and the facilities of steamboat navigation are then in perfection. We look forward with pleasure to the time when you will honor us with a visit.

There has nothing new or strange befallen us since I last wrote except the birth of a son which happened on the 21st of this month. Lucinda & he are both doing well. She had all things considered quite an easy labour although it lasted 24 hours. He is considered by most of folks as well as ourselves to be a "mighty pretty child" as they say in Illenois. He is quite fat, plump & lively & will weigh 6 or 7 pounds. Lucinda requests me to say that his name is John.[2]

I have been unwell for a day or two but at present am something better. I shall look for a letter from you soon.

H. Rutherford

1. The heavy rains would have contributed to the rapid spread of the wheat disease.

2. Dr. Rutherford is apparently underplaying the significance of the birth of his first son. Lucinda's pregnancy had not been mentioned in earlier letters.

14. *Letter of Dr. Hiram Rutherford to John Bowman, November 24, 1844. Oakland.*

Dear Sir,

Amidst the causes of laying up winter provisions for family & cattle I at length take time to adress you a few lines concerning the past present & future. Of the past I may state that we are all well. John has florised wonderfully: five months have rolled over and he has 'grown & waxed strong.' Lucinda thinks him a prodigy. Lucinda has enjoyed good health excepting an attack of Dysentry 3 months ago & lately two chills of the third day ague.[1] For myself I have had no sickness at all. I was laid up a day or two with the colic in the summer which came from eating too much: at present I am perfectly hearty. I should have written sooner. We rec'd a letter from Brother Jackson informing us of what we did know; concerning the Philad. Riots together with a kind of dirge monody of his own composition of the <u>horrors</u> of the same, a picture which with a little alteration would do well to prepare a missionary for his labours amongst the savages of the South Seas.[2] He told us of what we did not know viz the wonderful increase in your family. Just think of it; three at a time[3]—why sir if you keep on; in a few years more you will have to do as the bees do in Illenois—swarm out & hive somewhere else. You must have been calculating on Clay's election & the supremacy of home manufacture under a protective Tariff[4]—as it is there is danger of a famine in the land. But keep a stiff upper lip—let Retrenchment and <u>Reform</u> be your motto and notwithstanding you are cooped up between mountains with little elbow room to moove in you may still find Lykens valley large enough for you and them too. If you was in Illenois

1. Because of poor sanitation and food storage, dysentery was a common complaint in nineteenth-century Illinois.

2. During the Philadelphia Riots of 1844 (also known as Native American Riots), American nativists attacked foreigners and Catholic churches. The riots occurred in May and June.

3. The triplets did not survive.

4. Clay's "American System" called for protective tariffs which would, he argued, benefit American manufacturers and also Western farmers.

it would make no difference. You could set your sprouts out on the vast Prairies where 'the shrill winds whistle free' and like the Bannian[5] tree you could see your own branches take root in the deep rich soil & florish around you with over-shadowing luxuriance.

In consequence of the heavy rains in the Spring and the fore part of Summer there was an unusual amount of sickness in Illenois. There was not more than usual in these parts. A few children died. But one grown person 'stept out' within the bounds of my jurisdiction. At present it is healthy. I have never seen half as little corn raised in this country. The wet season drown'd it out. It is worth 25 cts a bushel an unusual price. But little pork is fatted. Everybody expects to scratch over this winter as best they can, & hope for better prospects next year. I expect to collect but little money this winter.

Nov 25. Lucinda has missed her chill for today. The weather is cold; we had an eclipse of the moon yesturday evening.

Friend Clay has not been elected president. Jemmy O Poke swept this country like fire. I do not know the vote of Illenois but his majority is large.[6] By the returns of Dauphin County I perceive that Lykens valley has given a good Whig vote. Millersburg was quite strong. There must have been a change since I left. Halifax too was right side up for once. Your neighbor J. C. Harper has got a seat in the great counsel house. Our friend Dr Rathbon fell far behind. He did but little in Paxton and in Mifflin his vote surprised me: what was the matter, was he too lazy to Electionere or what else.[7] Write soon and let me know. I suppose you begin to have some misgivings of the tenure of your valuable office. If you loose that I can see no remedy for you but the Retrenchment and reform before spoken of.

5. Banyan.

6. Dr. Rutherford, probably because he was an Abolitionist, does not seem to have been overly distressed by Clay's defeat in the presidential election of 1844. James K. Polk, Democrat, defeated Clay. Polk received 59,982 votes in Illinois and Clay, 45,931 votes.

7. The increase in Whig strength in Lykens Valley pleased Dr. Rutherford, and it is obvious that several of his friends in that area were politically active that year.

I would say in respect to the Lamps that the article sells pretty well provided the tubes are of the flat kind.[8] I do not think that much could be made on them. Common tin Lamps large size sell in the stores for 37 ½. I have no doubt but I could dispose of them & if Levi thinks proper to send them I shall do my best.[9] The freight & storage would on a couple of gross be 4 or 5 dollars. Direct to H Rutherford Oakland Coles Co Illenois

> (care of
> Burk & Co Pittsburg
> J M Stockwell Evansville
> J. Mc.Culloch Clinton
> Indiana)

When Lucinda will write I do not know. She has to answer Brother Jacksons kind letter. He enquired <u>anxiously</u> and affectionately how soon we would be back & to name an early day, without considering the folly of dropping all buissness every year or two to travel back 700 miles to say 'How do you do' & 'good bye'. God knows that if there was nobody else but him to see we should never think of crossing the mountains again. I shall expect a letter from you soon. Our best respects to your lady and particular love to your young Triumvers.

H. Rutherford

N. B. The cap sent in your letter came safe, it was rather small & John besides has never worn any, yet we hold it dear for the sake of the giver & may possibly use it on some of our forth comming responsibilities.

HR

15. *Letter of Lucinda Rutherford to Mrs. Frances Bowman, March 3, 1845. Oakland.*

Dear Mother,

Some time has elapsed since I have written to you, I intended writing long before this time, but from various causes have de-

---

8. John Bowman's letter concerning the sending of lamps to Oakland has not survived, and it is not possible to determine what kind of lamp is being discussed.

9. Levi was the brother of Lucinda Rutherford and John Bowman.

fered untill the present, you will please excuse my long delay in writing. Our little John grows very fast, plump and fat, he was born the 21 of last June, is now 8 months old, and never has had any sickness of account, he sets alone, and is beginning to get up at the chairs, he is the very resemblance of his dad, he is getting very interesting, and is a great deal of company for me. We have had a very favourable winter, and a fair prospect of an early spring, there has been but 3 or 4 real cold days and some little snow, but it soon passed away. It has been unusualy sickly in Illinois, last season and very fatal. The doctor is haveing a stable built to be completed this comeing summer, he talks of building a house in a year or two. We have a little girl living with us, she is 13 years of age, she does nearly all of our house work, we expect to keep her untill she is of age.[1] I am about to begin makeing a carpet, and shall be obliged to put in cotton chain as toe is very scarce here.[2] I have not quilted the flier quilt yet, but expect to have it quilted this summer, the red star quilt is not finished yet.

I am as yet very well pleased with the country, and I think I should be entirely contented, if you were here with us, I feel very anxious to see you and all the family and all the friends of old Millersburg. This is a splendid country to live in, we have our hazel thickets, where the nuts grow by thousands, and acers of plum trees, which will soon be in full bloom. We want for nothing but the friends we left behind. We have no cradle for little John, just rock him backwards and forewards in a common chair according to the custom of the country. I should like you to see John, he is such a sweet little chap. The doctor has entered some land and intends improving it, about 80 acers. I enjoy good health at present, I did occasionly have the chills, but lately they have entirely disapeared. The Doctor enjoys excellent health, he is busily engaged spliting rails to fence his land.[3]

1. The thirteen-year-old servant was still employed by the Rutherfords at the time of Lucinda's death.

2. *Toe*, i.e., *Tow*, is flax or hemp fiber prepared for spinning.

3. Dr. Rutherford became a large land owner, purchasing Congress land at $1.25 an acre, or semi-improved land, also inexpensive, from "rolling stones" who wanted to cross the Mississippi and head farther West.

We received a letter from brother John a few weeks since informing that you were all well, which I was gratified to hear. I received a few lines from Mary Frances,[4] it was written, and composed, admirably well. We have preaching here but once a month, and sometimes not that often, the Cumberland Presbyteriens. There is no Methodists in this place, there is a Methodist society about 4 miles from here, I have been there several times.

I was at a sugar camp last week, the sugar trees have spiles in them and a little troff setting under to catch the water, they had a kettle full boiling. I eat of it untill I was near about sick, there is a great deal of the home made sugar and molasses used in this country, I am very fond of both. We received a letter from Mr. Jackson some months since, he informed us of the Philadelphia riots, he also informed us that Margaret[5] had three babies at one birth, but did not mention that they were dead. I was surprised to hear they were all dead, and that they lived so short a time.

I cannot tell how soon we will visit you, I expect it will be before a great while, the doct. promised that after we are here 3 years he would take me back, I intend to hold him to his bargain, I should be pleased to see some of you in Illenois.

I must bring my letter to a conclusion as it is 12 o clock at night. Pleas excuse my composition and all mistakes as I am a poor hand at writing letters, give love to Johns family. My love to all inquireing Friends.

The Doctor and John joins me in love. I will write to you again, to you and the boys

> From your affectionate Daughter
> Lucinda Rutherford

16. *Letter of Dr. Hiram Rutherford to John Bowman, June 24, 1845.
Oakland.*

Dear Sir

Yours has just been received and contrary to custom I answer

4. Unidentified, but probably a young relative.
5. John Bowman's wife.

it in unusual quick time. Lucinda &c have gone a visiting & I am left alone with nothing to do which suits my inclination to perform except to write you a letter. We have had in this country rather a dry winter & spring. In these parts the crops look fine. The Black birds destroyed great quantities of corn. We have not had any dry weather to do damage. The corn looks fine. I have a patch of corn & potatoes that are verry promising, particularly the latter. I had potatoes on the same ground last year—the tops grew from 5 to 9 feet long, roots in <u>proportion</u>. This year they look even better than last. However when I take off the crops I will give you an account of them. For the last week we have had pretty steady rain. With you the weather has been excessively dry. I remember in 38 there was the driest season I ever knew in Penn—in 41 we had a wonderful dry time in Illenois. Still good crops considering were raised. Illenois is said by some to be the hottest, the coldest, the wettest & the driest country in the United States. Still crops seldom fail, especialy from drought. The soil is so deep that vegitation cannot burn out.

I am glad you have resolved to make a trip to the west. How glad we shall be to see you. In this country our eyes are never greeted by any body we have ever seen before. If you ever come out here what a contrast, our immense plains blooming with the richest verdue will be, to the barren hills of Lykens Valley. Still I can scarce beleive that you would 'settle'—it is a principle of mans nature that the more barren & unkind the soil on which he is raised; the stronger is his attatchment to it—and you I beleive would not be an exception—however fairly you might be located in the west, the flesh pots of Egypt would expand & grow in the memory—Old Lykens with its <u>inteligent</u> inhabitants an Elyssium in Retrospection; and of consequence a discontent with the present would follow. But enough of this? Come out & see us. I should be happy to see you at any time, but spring exhibits the country best. Then come next spring & I will take a trip with you to the Lead Mines of Illenois and Wisconsin. Thos Huchison lives there.[1] That Region is possessed of a good soil

1. Galena, Illinois, was a major center of the Illinois-Wisconsin lead mining area. Thomas Hutchison (or Huchison) was from Goods Mill, and in his letter

and the mineral does and always will make it a good market. Thousands of cattle are annualy driven there from Middle & Southern Illenois. You talk of Oregon. I suppose you have not seen the report to the last congress on that subject. That report was partial, & urged immediate occupation. Still all the tillable land estimated by it in that territory, of 500 000 square miles, amounts to but 14 millions of acres a little more than half the size of Illenois.[2] Calafornia is now beginning to lead the emigrating sperit. Afterwards some oasis twill probably be found in the great American Desert[3], or amidst the Esquimaux & white bears of the Polar circle. Texas has had its day, Iowa (which is a realy good country) has had its fill & now the race is for Oregon & California.

We are in usual health. John is beginning to whistle & walk. There is no prospects of Margarets wishes for our family being fulfilled. We have concluded to pospone that affair for a year or so yet.[4] Remember us to all our friends <u>H. Rutherford</u>

Let us hear from you soon. I cannot close w'out expressing our thanks for papers, pamphlets &c received from you.

17. *Letter of Dr. Hiram Rutherford to John Bowman, October 14,*
1845. Oakland.

Dear Brother
My right to use the foregoing title has passed away; and al-

---

of March 10, 1841, to Bowman, Dr. Rutherford had asked about the Hutchisons. The Hutchisons had obviously moved West, and Dr. Rutherford was proposing a visit.

2. Oregon fever was particularly strong at this time. In the winter of 1842–43, Congress printed 5,000 copies of *Extracts from the Report of Lieutenant Wilkes to the Secretary of the Navy, of the Examination of the Oregon Territory*, a report which greatly increased interest in settling that territory. Dr. Rutherford's figures on the size of Oregon were probably from contemporary newspapers. Dr. Rutherford stayed in Oakland for sixty years and was bemused by the rush to Oregon, California, Texas, and Iowa.

3. Between 1820 and 1850, many maps labelled the area from the Mississippi west to the Rocky Mountains as "The Great American Desert."

4. The Rutherfords had decided to postpone the conception of another child. Dr. Rutherford does not indicate what birth control methods were being used.

though now for the first time I use it, yet I hope you will permit me to call you so, for the sake of her who was your sister and my wife. I perceive by yours of Sept 20th that you was ignorant of Lucinda's death: but a few days later & you must have heard the melancholy news. Oh what a shock you must have felt, but I cannot tell you the pain it was, of communicating to your mother, the sad tidings of our misfortune. That sad duty I would gladly have avoided, had not honor compelled me to perform the task.

When I wrote to your mother I beleive I stated that I would detail to you, the circumstances of Lucindas illness. The Methodist Society in this neighborhood, hold camp meetings every 2 years, about 3½ miles distant from this town. The first year we came out she attended one—staid one night at the camp & was attacked by a violent fever directly afterwards. This year it was for a while deemed too sickly to hold one, but by the urgent entreaties of the circuit preacher a meeting was held at which more than fifty persons took sick & the congregation prematurely broke up.[1] Lucinda was exceedingly anxious to attend, & knowing my opposition to such collections of people, proposed attending on Sunday only. But I knowing how much it would gratify her, had her taken there on Saturday, to stay till Sunday evening. She promised not to stay nor lodge on the camp ground at night, but to put up with a particular friend close at hand. I could not well be there with her. Sickness was raging like a devouring element all over the country. I was called every where, & night & day alike found me posting from house to house. I found leisure to spend ½ an hour on Sunday afternoon (Aug 31st) at the camp. She immediately told me that she had staid all night in a tent: that some men occupied the raised beds, & she & some other women lay on some straw on the ground, and was anxious to know if I was angry. I told her I was sorry but she said that they persuaded her to stay and that she did not like to speak for a raised bed; most of the guests were strangers. I had charged her by no means to sleep on the ground for by

1. The name of the circuit preacher is never mentioned in the letter, nor is he identified in Dr. Rutherford's later accounts of religion in Oakland.

doing so she took her first fever two years ago. Lucindas frank nature never allowed her to conceal from me any fault, which she thought she had committed, or withold any thing from me for a moment, which she considered my right to know. She then asked my permision to have John babtised which was done. I then left & did not get home till past midnight. She returned late. Some of her friends tried to persuade her to stay all night, & when she would not, they were long in bringing her horse, her company from this place had left, she carried the child herself & it was an hour after sundown before she got home.

I think the seccond day afterwards, she complained of a pain in her right armpit. She continued to work till thursday when it became agravated by quilting at a neighbors. She then carried her arm in a sling. About Sunday she took a chill; the arm swelled considerably but never showed any appearance of gathering. The fever was moderate. The pains extended into her breast which was blistered, without releif. Opium affected her head so much that she could use but little of it. Poultices did not releive her arm. I still had no idea that her danger was so great, for when I could be with her she complained little.[2] But death was doing his work & I did not know it. On the morning of the 12th the conviction of her great danger first broke on my mind & in my distress I burst into tears. She then began to speak of death, of prayr, of her soul and of her mother. I asked her why she thought she would die. She said it was because I had given her up. I thought she would last 2 or 3 days, & I hoped that a favourable turn might yet take place. Oh it is hard to beleive that so dear an object would die: to die and leave me forever. I soothed her, & told her that I thought she would yet get well— that my distress was for her sufferings. She kept comparatively strong all day. When hope was no more I could not tell her that she would die. I have often pronounced that word to the dying, with but little emotion; but to her I could not say it. I had brought her to a far country there to die amidst strangers; & no mother or brother to weep over her passing sperit. I only was there to comfort her, with all these sad reflections on my mind.

2. The exact nature of Lucinda's illness is not known.

Her breath became shorter, her mind wandered & I could hear her sometimes say she would die. Her last hour was restless on account of the difficult breathing, but this left her & she sunk quietly in death about 8 o clock in the evening. She was buried the next evening. I could get no preacher to attend her funeral, all was sick but two kind neighbors performed that service. A hymn was sung and an affecting prayr was made ere the ground closed over her forever. Oh there was much consolation in that prayer, although [I was] a solitary mourner, the young & old who kneeled around the grave could then join me in my sorrow and the companionship of gref lightened the burden on my own head. I have a great many sad reflections on this subject. I know your kind nature will not misapprehend me. I was too blind to her danger. I was not with her enough. Every body was sick. Such a distressing time has never before been known in the West. The calls were incessant & I often went when I should have staid by her side. There are a thousand things I could say concerning her last illness, and her health for the last year, were you here, or I there with you. You spoke of coming out, do so, visit me & with me let us kneel over her grave. Our son has been sick, he took remitting fever, which declined into chills. It is five or six days since he last had them; he looks hearty & well. I am still keeping house. I have taken in a young man & wife. The girl we have had since spring, is still with me. John is living with a widdow woman close by. Whether I shall bring him home or not, I have not yet determined. Sickness this year as I said before, has been without a paralel. It commenced in the beginning of August to be bad and continued unabated throughout Sept. While Lucinda lay a corpse great numbers came, not knowing my misfortune for attendance & medicine. They did not let me rest, the night after her funeral, I had to get up at 2 o clock & ride till 12 at night, I did not get more than 3 hours sleep out of the 24 & sometimes not one. In the first week after her death I have never seen such a time for sickness. My buissness this season has nearly doubled any other since I am in this state.

Tell your mother that I am looking for a letter from her every mail. Should she neglect me I shall ever be wretched. I know that she blames me for taking her daughter from her to a dis-

tant country but she cannot blame or reproach me worse than I
do myself. Tell her to write, let it be what it will. I will take in
kindness the heaviest reproaches she can put on me. Remember
me to your family, your brothers & sisters, write to me soon.

Lucinda cannot join with me in love to you and yours again,
but her sperit in heaven no doubt dwells on us in its godly ocu-
pation for as she was kind and good here she is not less so there.

H. Rutherford

18. *Letter of Dr. Hiram Rutherford to Mrs. Frances Bowman,*
January 4, 1846. Oakland.

Honored Mother,

Yours of Dec 2 was received two or three weeks ago, and
would have been attended to immediately had I not thought,
that it required a mature, decided, and deliberate answer. When
I wrote to yourself and John, I was urgent for you to write. In
my distress I stated that I had manifold reflections on that sad
event, and however much you might reproach me that the
epistle would be received as a favor with submission and pleasure. Honored mother I hereby acknowledge the recipt of your
letter, and although its contents gives me a great deal of Pain
and distress, yet from my heart I thank you. Your silence would
have been much more intollerable, and in duty and inclination,
I bow my head in submission to your displeasure.

I did not receive Johns letter till two days after mine to him
had gone east. I have since delayed writing thinking he would
write again. In that letter he stated your wish to have the body
of Lucinda removed from hence to Millersburg. I thought from
his language, that he made the request in compliance with your
wish—a wish which could not see the difficulties, which his own
good judgment taught him lay in the way. Please considder
some of these difficulties. I live 145 miles from the Ohio River.
The road thence is always bad. It crosses several large swamps
and three Rivers. The journey thence east would be steamboat
and canal conveyance, which might be effected easily enough
provided the corpse was not in a decaying condition. Such a trip

would cost me two or three months time. The loss to my buissness and the expences would be more than $300. My abilities to perform this work are ample, and you may say why not do it. It is but 40 miles to the Wabash River and a boat might be taken there. It is true the Wabash is a large stream, and when high can be navigated 200 miles, but it seldom rises sufficient for certain navigation till June.

You urge me to leave here, that I may die out here too; well mother, if such is the will of God I hope I shall meet the King of terrors prepared or unprepared without a murmur. I do not expect old age to bless my head. The loborious buissness which I follow attended as it is with such great exposures, must ere many years wear down my frame. But if my days are to be short (and I have a presentiment that so it will be) I know that here I can soon attain Independence, and leave something for our son to begin the world with. I expect to remain in this country, and probably die here, when that time comes I wish to lie by Lucinda's side. Therefore her body will lie in the wilderness under the broad armed oak, or if I leave, it shall go with me, be the place of my destination, whither soever it may be. Should I remoove to the east, I shall take it with me, not to lay it in Millersburg but with my fathers in Paxton Church yard, with whom may God allow me to rest my bones in peace. You have my answer.

I considder your proposal to take care of our son as made, more in the sperit of kindness than with any expectation of its being complied with. Certainly you would not expect me to part from him, you know full well the relations of parent and child: I have him at home with me. I have taken a young couple into the house with me, and retain the services of the girl we had before Lucindas death as a nurse. I have engaged these persons for a year. John is well, he is now sitting at my feet with his toys. The bloom has returned to his cheek and he looks I think beautiful. When I again visit Penna. I shall take him with me of course. But when that time will be circumstances must determine, which will render it uncertain when you shall see Lucindas child.

Lucinda enjoyed frequent oppertunities of hearing the gospel from her own denomination. Since early last Spring there has been preaching every month at our house. The circuit preacher was with us a week or so since & stayed a couple of days. I showed him your letter. He judged you to be a Presbyterian much to my surprise. You do not beleive that she received injury at the camp meeting and that the carrying of the child hurt her. It may be as you think. I drew the inferance from former facts. Two years ago she returned from meeting with the fever. This time the disease attacked her arm, the one upon which she lay. A woman does not usually carry her child on the right arm on horseback. You say she should have had every attention. I agree with you there, and in sorrow. She cannot rise from the grave and speak in my behalf. I was blinded to her danger, and O how bitter is the reflection that I did not do all I might have done, had I apprehended her critical situation. The love I bore her might speak in my behalf, but perhaps you cannot see things in that light. You honored Mother once lost a husband, and it is probable when you look back from your first connection with him till its close in death, that you cannot remember a single act towards him to cause you regret, or a single duty unperformed. 'Tis true you had no public cares to distract your attention, nor like me hundreds of fellow citizens calling for your services. Let anyone, placed in my situation, who had nerve enough to resist the universal cry of distress, be accounted as a superior being— let him say to his fellows, 'Stand aside, I am holier than thou.'

You say you are all verry sorry that you let her leave you. On that point you should not reflect upon yourselves, you could not prevent it, I was never aware till the day of her death, how much you opposed her going with me. At that time, when I first saw the reality of her situation, I burst into tears. She spoke to me in all the sweetness of her nature. 'Honey I beleive I must die, I am affraid I am not well enough prepared. I have been wicked, and a death bed is unfitted for prayr.' She said this slowly while sitting alone in the bed. She then added 'Mother told me before we married, that I would follow you and loose my own soul.' It had been my design to talk with her on the prospects of a future state. But after that, I could not mention it more, I told her to lie down and not think of such sad things, that I was distressed to see her suffer, and that I thought she would soon be better. To die so far from her people was as you say distressing. Her who had pronounced the curse which lay upon her soul, was not with her to remoove the load, or aswage the bitterness of death. Mother let us weep, I as I write, you as you read these lines. When we meet again we will talk these things over, for at present my heart is full and poor wicked sinful man as I am, may God have mercy on my Soul. I will probably have an oppertunity in the Spring of sending you some of her clothes. They hang just where she last put them with her own hands. I have not had heart to disturb them.

I am looking anxiously for a letter from John, if he has not written when you receive this, tell him that I wish him to state, whether he regrets Lucindas union with me, for you say you <u>all</u> do, and whether he thinks that Death might not strike his victims in Lykens Valley, as well as in Illenois.

You seem to have been under a wrong impression as to our returning in two years. I distinctly stated to some of your family, John, Margaret, Josiah &c that we would not be back for four years, and from my first interview with Lucinda after my return I never gave her any hopes of revisiting her friends sooner than that time. You cannot imagine how deranging it is to buissness like mine an abscence of 3 or 4 months produces. Do not forget me but write again

I remain your wretched son
H. Rutherford

19. *Letter of Dr. Hiram Rutherford to John Bowman, April 26, 1846. Oakland.*

Dear Brother

Your last has been duly received and I assure you that I felt the most profound grattitude on receiving [it,] on taking it from the office I saw the well known hand & I knew that me and mine were not forgotten. Mothers letter I confess distressed me much & your not answering the request I made in my reply increased my gloom greatly. I began to consider it to be true that <u>you</u>, as well as all (as represented in mothers letter) regretted the comittal of a sister to my care. My mind became so disturbed that had I not received your letter when I did the next mail would have contained one for you asking your mind upon that melancholy subject. I feel greatful to the giver of all good that your mind has been disposed to look upon this subject in a candid and sensible way. We often think that were our lives to be lived again on earth that we would mend many acts which we look upon with regret. If your own wife were taken from you you would be happier than I am if you could call to mind no act or circumstance (trivial in themselves) which you would not look upon with sorrow. I married Lucinda because I loved her. And he who sits on high knows that that flame can live for one and one alone. No one knew that fact better than she did. She was dutiful, and never ceased her endeavors to please me, may her reward be great. She was anxious as well as myself to become independent of the world and leave a competence for our son. We were prosperous but death came as a theif in the night and destroyed all our hopes. I do not regret that we married, far from it, nor do I regret that I brought her here. But there are many things which I do regret—Thoughtless and hasty words spoken & forgotten recur to mind but above all, that I did not see her danger in her last illness. How unfortunate I sometimes think that if I had bled her largely at the start possibly she would have recovered but her disease never assumed an alarming stage till no remedy would avail. As you say these regrets are a matter for my own concience. So be it. God have mercy on my soul. As to Mother, commend me to her, when her and I meet again perhaps we will understand each other better. In two years if God spares us I shall show her Lucindas child. My own dear son, he is now by my side in blooming health, pray with me that God may spare him a life for his wretched fathers sake, and that his mother may still live in him to comfort my declining years.

You say it is necessary for me to appoint a guardian for John. I would name your brother Levi if you have no objections with this proviso to endeavor to loan the money out at 6 percent and make it accumulate as much as it can. Money here brings from

6 to 10 percent readily. Also I do not know whether as guardian he could remove John from my care, if so the appointment is withdrawn.[1] Otherways I should be glad if he would accept the trust as Lucinda bore testimony that he loved her well.

I should be pleased to see you here. I think it would be for your profit to visit the west, it would gratify me much, & you could then judge for yourself. If you were here I could live with you & I should feel much happier with those near & dear to me.

H. Rutherford

Let me hear from you soon, how glad I would be to see you. There is none here to whom I can call brother. I learn from home that my oldest sister is labouring under cancer & that her days are nearly finished. Such my friend is Mortality. Let us think of ourselves and O may our garments be white & our lamps lit as we approach after the bridegroom the doors of eternal life.

HR

20. *Letter of Dr. Hiram Rutherford to John Bowman, November 30, 1846. Oakland.*

Dear Brother
The inteligence contained in your last letter, of Mothers death is truly surprising. If it was unexpected to you, it was much more so to me. How true it is that in the midst of life, we are equaly so in the midst of Death. And although many years had gathered on her honored brow, and the moniter Time had bid us expect that eternity for her was near; yet what a cold shock is produced upon us, when Death claims his own. We probably feel the visitation more keenly in proportion to the suddenness of the bereavement. In memory I can see her still, when she

1. Obviously some money was passing from Lucinda's estate in Pennsylvania to John Rutherford. Dr. Rutherford was willing to have Lucinda's brother named guardian on condition that John could not be removed from his father's care. Mrs. Bowman had wanted to take the boy, and Dr. Rutherford was being cautious about legal technicalities.

wrung my hand for the last time; when Lucinda left her home to return no more forever. She thought, as I do, that I should have seen my dear wifes approaching end sooner than I did. But it was otherwise ordered. I was blind & could not perceive the cloud of death suspended over her. Mothers end is a similar example. The one died in the land of the Stranger, with no friend near but poor sinful me—the other in the midst of her children; without at least some of them knowing that her time had so suddenly come. But my dear Brother a just God will take care of his own. 'I am the good shepherd, I know my masters sheep, and no man shall deliver them out of my hands.'[1] Ere this their sperits may have mingled in eternity, to wait for those they love to join with them in anthems on high.

To me this melancholy event was totaly unthought of, I had calculated that within 18 months I should present to her our child. I have often imagined to myself the joy she would feel on first beholding his blooming face, when she would first clasp to her bosom Lucinda's child. It was my design to gratify her with his picture. A few weeks before I rec'd your letter, a person staid here a few days who took likenesses by the Daugorreotype process. But the weather was cloudy & I could not get it taken.—[2]

How often have I wished for a likeness of Lucinda. It would be a solace to a Sperit, which with her lies buried deep in the ground. But O Brother eternity is coming on us all. A few more years & our forms now strong in life, will be quiet & still. My Father has completed his three score years & ten. Mother verges close to that limit of human life. My brother Abner writes that they look well & hearty. But the Son of Man cometh as a theif in the night, and it often fills my heart with distress, to think that I may never see their faces again.

1. John 10: 14–15: "I am the good shepherd, and know my *sheep*, and am known of mine. As the Father knoweth me, even so know I the Father: and I lay down my life for the sheep."

2. Traveling daguerreotypists were common at this time. Daguerre had introduced his photographic process in France in 1839, and it was quickly introduced into America. Sunlight was needed for the process, and in the early years, the exposure time was long.

But not to anticipate trouble, permit me to recur for a few moments to the past, as this occasion naturaly brings it to mind. When first my fireside became desolate, my brothers sympathised with me. They are kind affectionate men, but Lucinda was measurably a stranger to them, they could not know her as you & I did. I could not open my bosom to them as I could to you, and although a wicked unregenerate man, may not call down a blessing upon your house for the comfort you have afforded him; yet permit him to beleive, that the bonds of affection & kindred still stands strong between us, endeared by my child and hallowed by the memory of her who lies deep in the ground—Her grave is in the deep wild wood, the broad armed oak waves over her—the roses of a summer have bloomed above her head. But O Brother what a solemn place the last house of the living is. Should you ever come to Illenois your heart can feel with mine by that hallowed ground, that the Lord giveth & the Lord taketh away blessed be the name of the Lord.

But let us be calm again. Many in this world are worse off than we. My home is desolate, my son is with the lady I spoke of in my last letter. I have quit house keeping and board out as in former years. Still I have some comforts. My buissness has been profitable & I am independent in a pecuniary point of view. I have some calculations visiting you in the spring of 1848. My brother Abner writes that he expects to visit Illenois next spring or summer. Possibly you may resolve to do so too. I should have written a week sooner but I received a severe injury to the mid finger of my right hand in raising my new house.

I desire that Levi may be appointed guardian to John as soon as convenient. Tell him that his ward is hearty, lively, active and speaks quite plain.

There is at present in this place 1 tavern, 1 grocery, 3 stores, 1 blacksmith, 1 waggonmaker, 2 carpenters, 1 lawyer, and 2 doctors.

Remember me affectionately to your wife & children, Josiah, Levi, & Emeline.

I remain your Brother & Friend
H. Rutherford

21. *Letter of Dr. Hiram Rutherford to John Bowman, July 7, 1847. Oakland.*

Dear Brother

It is with pleasure that I am enabled to assure you of the continued good health of your little namesake my son. He is ruged & hearty. My own health for nearly a year has been but indifferent. In May last I went into the water to fish & have felt like a new man ever since. However the sickly season is comming on, and I may, from unavoidable exposure be again laid on my back as I was last season.

I percive by your letter that considerable buissness is expected to be carried on in your country when the improvements are finished. I doubt not that you are improving your circumstances by the operation. I recd a letter not long since from Esq Seal. He tells me that one of his girls ran off & married against his will—that Novinger is dead-done with electionering, and that J Shaefer lives at the point. Tell me how he & his wife gets along, what family they have &c.[1]

I am sorry to hear of Mrs Jacksons illness. I hope she is again in health. Lucinda always spoke of her with the tenderest affection. Levi & Emeline I presume are still in Millersburg. Josiah is no doubt at his old occupation. I perceive that no guardian as yet has been appointed for John & that you expect that it may do as well to have it deferred till next spring. I doubt not that you have good reasons for postponing the appointment. But as a favor I would be pleased to know whether you calculate on allowing any percentage for the use of the money belonging to him in your possession.[2] All things of earth are uncertain more or less. I may not see Lykens valey next spring as I would wish; perhaps I may never see it again. For my sons sake I have long kept my buissness as square as possible lest I might be required

1. The letter from Seal is not in the Rutherford papers, and Seal, Novinger, and Shaefer cannot be identified. The references do indicate Dr. Rutherford's continued interest in his Lykens Valley acquaintances.

2. Dr. Rutherford is suggesting that interest on money from Lucinda's estate should be paid to John Rutherford.

to go back to dust by the side of his mother. I enclose you a portion of a letter which I recd from my sister Sarah Kendig a few days after the last letter I wrote you. I do this that you may see her own words, concerning a call she made upon Mother a year ago. The person described as 25 or 30 years of age I supposed to be Levi, the other Benjamin. The call was made at my particular request & I assure you, that I never felt more mortified in all my life than when I read the result. I endeavored to explain to her in return that Levi acted so from a natural aversion to converse with strangers. But the reason does not satisfy me. It may yet be in my power to do Benjamin a kindness for his conduct. May God bless him for it.

Yesterday I visited Lucinda's grave. The rose bushes which I planted 16 months ago were in bloom. I enclose a couple of the male flowers as the female are nearly white & not so pretty. One is taken from her head, the other from her feet. The rose is peculiar to this country. Many people ornament their yards and gardens with it. I have always admired it above all other varieties of rose. It will bloom throughout this month and a thousand flowers will fall around where Lucinda lies. I left that holy place with a lighter heart than I ever did before. If these specimens should preserve well give one to Emeline & the other to Mrs Jackson to look upon for their sisters sake.

On Saturday last, 3d inst., I attended a celebration & free dinner, given by the citizens of the county at the county seat, to the heroes of Cerro Gordo:[3] 30 or 40 paraded from this county. About 1200 ladies were present & probably 2000 men. A 6 pounder made the air on these prairies vibrate for 20 miles. In the evening the public square was illuminated & about 60 ladies & gentlemen 'Tript the light fantastic toe,' on the green, amongst the ornamental trees. Before midnight the dancers adjourned & the celebration closed for 1847.

Once I was fond of such amusements. I have no objection to them still. But since my marriage I have never danced but once.

---

3. The Cerro Gordo battle took place April 18, 1847, in the interior of Mexico. General Winfield Scott's army defeated General Santa Anna's troops.

Remember me to your wife & children. Forget not your brother in misfortune, but write soon. Delay not so long as formerly. I remain your brother

H. Rutherford

p.s. The corn crops are splendid. The winter crops are verry light. I have 8 acres of excellent wheat which I shall probably cut tomorrow. Cattle are high, 3 year old steers are worth 17$, cows 9 or 10, stock hogs 2½ to 3$ per hundred gross, mule colts 20$.

—I have long quit housekeeping. I board with the people I first lived with. I have my office & bed in my own house & stay in it alone. John is still with his foster mother Mrs. Black; he is wearing pants, is 3 feet 2 inches high & active as a cat. My expenses are $1 per week for him $1.50 for my self for boarding. I have 2 horses, one of which I had with me when in Pennsylvania. He was Lucindas favorite steed. He carried her to & from that fatal camp ground.

Letter of Mrs. Kendig to Dr. Hiram Rutherford, December 11, 1846. Middletown. Enclosed in Letter 21.

I suppose you have heard of the Death of your Mother-in-law. I have not heard any of the particulars of her Death than she died of Inflamation of the Bowels. Last summer I think in July I was up at Sally Allens. I went up in the boat and took Clara and Marion our babe with me. Kendig came up with the carriage for us and on our way down we passed through Millersburg, it was just evening and we wanted to go to Halifax. Whilst our horses were watering I took Clara and went up to Mrs. Bowmans. I told her who I was. She treated me very well, but seemed very reserved in her manners; I thought her a very nice old lady. I met two of her sons, on the porch, the elder appeared to be a man of about 25 or 30, he seemed to be very dry indeed, and paid no attention to me scarcely. The younger one looked like a boy of 17 or 18, a very pleasant, agreeable boy, and seemed disposed to be friendly. . . .

22. *Letter of Dr. Hiram Rutherford to John Bowman, October 25,*
1847. Oakland.

Dear Brother

Yours of 3rd Sept is before me. I hope that the bodily ailings which you mention are neither serious nor permanent. Last Spring I feared much for my own health during the present summer but those anticipations have been agreeably disappointed. Except for a few attacks of diarrhea (a complaint to which I am very subject) I have enjoyed good health and at present feel perfectly well. John has had no sickness; and for more than a year has not swallowed a dose of medicine. The present season has been unusualy healthy. But one death has occured in my practice; and that one was attended to with peculiar distress to her family and pain to myself. The wife of a gentleman (Mr Sargent) was taken early in July with a severe attack of fever. I had attended her several times previously, and knew well her weakly constitution. She was most carefully treated and the disease began to abate. But as bodily strength returned the mental faculties gave way. She who had led a most exemplary life, conceived her sins to be greater than she could bear. She managed singularly enough to get hold of some arsenic, and took a fatal portion. She concealed the fact too long for releif, and the best woman on the Ambraw sunk into the grave an involuntary suicide. The deceased was my wifes most particular friend, and as I stood by her & saw her last breath, the reccollection of their intimacy called forth the first tears I have shed for mortal since Lucinda died.[1]

As to the guardianship of John I do not wish any thing of the kind entered into at present. I neglected in my last letter to recal

1. For a moving sketch of Mrs. Sargent, see pt. 2, art. 2.

the appointment I had made, I did not think of it till I had sealed it, but considered that under the circumstances there detailed you would act as you have. In all probability I shall be with you in April or May next. This determination may be altered, as I expect my youngest brother to be with me in about a week from this time, but it is highly probable that should we live, John & myself will be with you in the spring.

By the last mail I received a letter from my brother the Doctor.[2] It appears he has been visited by Mr Berryhill who it also appears is attorney to our worthy brother Mr Jackson. Mr Jackson it seems doubts your honesty, so much that he is about to institute proceedings to compel the settlement of your fathers estate. Mr Jacksons organ of marvelousness is no doubt a predominant feature of his character. My brother says he expects to convict you of embezzlement to a great amount, and his attorney urges me to open a correspondence with Mr Jackson on the subject. As the settlement of that estate never troubled me, I do not think I shall at this late time of day, join myself with Mr J. in a crusade against you. If I could give what little is there belonging to my son away, I would freely do it. There are those of your family whom I beleive would need it much more than he ever will.

Our circuit court sat last week. I had the pleasure of attending as a party to give reasons why Justice should <u>not</u> be done. I was sued by a person named Matson for the gentlemanly sum of twenty five hundred dollars & 50 dol damage. The suit did not come on. My attorney submitted a plea of dismissal which was not decided and so it stands till May next.

The circumstances of this suit arose from the following occurrances. About 2 years ago Matson brought with him from Kentucky a free man and his wife & five children who were his Slaves there, to this county: and settled them on his farm 12 miles distant from this place. He suffered them to remain with him till last summer, when he determined to remove the children to his residence in Kentucky, and leave the old people childless in Illenois. He had previously taken back one child and

2. William Rutherford, the Harrisburg physician.

then resolved to remove the remaining 4. The parents to avoid force left his farm with their children, and came to this place, and put themselves under the protection of a man named Ashmore. Matson got out a process to take them as runaways, and the woman & children were brought before a court of 3 justices. A number of us feeling an interest in the case employed the Hon. O B Ficklin M. C. of this county to defend them. The court decided to commit them to jail, as runaways and it was concluded to try the case before the circuit Judge at the Oct.term. Matson sued Ashmore & myself for harboring them (the fine for which is $500. for each person by law). However the negroe trial came on, and the arguments were heard by two of our circuit Judges, who ordered them to be discharged from the custody of the Sherriff and Matson pay the costs, amounting to $200. Matson left next day for Kentucky without his blacks and whether he will return to attend to the suits against Mr Ashmore or myself in May is uncertain. Be it as it may I feel no uneasiness as I did not have them on my premises and besides I expect to get out of the suit from a defect in the declaration.

Please write soon. I am grateful for the news you give, pray continue to regard me as your brother.

H Rutherford

23. *Letter of Dr. Hiram Rutherford to John Bowman, February 7, 1848. Oakland.*

Dear Brother

Yours of Dec 23 came to hand at last. I confess that it appeared to be a great length of time from the date of my letter till yours was received. Yet I feel doubly thankful for the favor of your correspondence. First because I can write but little in return to interest you. You have no associations here local or personal to mingle with your feelings. All is blank and besides it is far away. Second for the pleasure your letters afford me. In them I see & hear my old companions as of yore: when we traded, sported, and spree'd together a period of my life but illy spent, though attended with many delightful rememberances.

I am glad to hear of your own health being amended as well as your wifes convalescence. I see you are still persuing the way of all flesh—well trot on: Laurance Sterne defines a good citizen, to be one, who has built a house, planted a tree and got a child.[1] You are in my opinion a verry good citizen, for Scripture says 'by their works ye shall know them.' I perceive that your pecuniary affairs are in a creditable condition which combined with circumstances of a wife & children should render you comfortable. May you live long to enjoy it. Allow me to give you a synopsis of my life for the last two years and upwards. After my wifes death I continued house keeping a year at a great expense. I did this that I might keep my child with me but my house keepers were too young to attend to such buissness & I was constantly fearful of some accident happening to him, as the sickly season of 46 came on I removed him to my neighbor Mrs Black (a most worthy woman) where he still continues. In the fall I broke up and took another family into the house, with whom I boarded till spring. I then moved my bags & baggage into my new house and have boarded at various places since. Since I removed last spring I have had no family with me, I tread my halls alone, make my bed & sleep alone. My house cost me somewhat over 1600$. I built it to please myself and of course it took money to do it. I own 180 acres of land & shall put up another building next spring or summer to rent. Last summer a botanic physician stopped here; he did some buissness, but was taken in the fall with Typhoid Fever and died.[2] Since then my old competitior has pulled up stakes. His health being in a declining condition unsuited to a laborious practice. He left a few days ago for Ohio. I alone am left for this large tract of country. I expect some one will speedily drop in but duty and interest requires me to stick well to my place. I expect my cousin Levi

1. Laurence Sterne (1713–1768), English novelist, was most famous in nineteenth-century America for *The Life and Opinions of Tristram Shandy*. We have been unable to identify this quotation.

2. The botanic physician used herbs and steam baths in his treatments. The botanic system could easily be followed by those without a medical education. Dr. Rutherford clearly had little regard for this irregular system and its practitioners.

Rutherford in the spring; he is now attending Medical Lectures at Philad. Whether he will locate here or not is uncertain. I think I shall not be East the comming spring, besides it is probable that I may marry again; if so, like the guest bidden to the feast, I cannot come.[3] My youngest brother was out to see me in November. He did not stay but a couple of weeks. He was making a protracted journey through the western states—he is probably at home by this time. His visit gratified me much. It has been a great consolation to me in my domestic affliction that my brothers as well as yourself have given me repeated proofs of affection. I shall appoint my brother John P Rutherford guardian for my son, with whom you will settle Lucindas account. I shall send him a bill of it which she brought with her. If John does not accept Abner probably will. My son is in excellent health. He has not taken a dose of medicine for more than a year. My own health is better than usual. This I attribute to the comfort of my lodging place. I occupy my best parlor and can go to sleep of a cold night with a comfortable fire blazing on the hearth. I have taken some precautions to avoid the Quinsey (my old enemy).[4] I wear a high heavy stock which I had of you but never used till the present winter. I have for the first time allowed the hair to grow unshaven on my throat and jaws. I feel well and you would find me if you were here as robust as I ever was. The winter has been mild. I hope your location in Millersburg will be agreeable and profitable to you. As you pledged yourself in your last to write soon again I shall close with the prayer that your wrath against our worthy Brother of the City may abate. Remember the greatest of virtues is Charity, and where much is

3. Dr. Rutherford's second wife, Harriet Hutcherson, was born in 1826 in Kentucky, the daughter of Thomas and Catherine Hutcherson. The Hutchersons moved to Springfield, Illinois, in 1830 and at one time owned the land where Lincoln is now buried. Dr. Rutherford met Harriet Hutcherson in 1847 during the *Matson* slave trial; Miss Hutcherson was visiting her cousin, Mrs. Fannie Van Meter, wife of Dr. Samuel Van Meter, a Charleston physician. Dr. Rutherford and Miss Hutcherson were married in April of 1848. She took over the care of Lucinda's son, helped her husband compound his medicine, took in two black waifs, and reared her own seven children who survived infancy. Like her husband, she was active in community affairs. She died in 1914.

4. Sore throat.

needed much should be <u>given</u>—it covereth a multitude of sins. My love to you & yours

H. Rutherford

Dr. Hiram Rutherford as a young man. *Courtesy, Landmarks, Inc.*

Nov. 7. Lectures by Doctor Dunglisson.

Professor in Jefferson Medical College of Institutes of Medicine & Medical Jurisprudence

1836

Lecture 1st. Bile in the Stomach

It is no proof of bile being in the stomach, in an undue quantity, from the fact, that in vomiting by antimonial Emetics, a large quantity of it is often discharged. The movement of the contents of the stomach in vomiting is retrograde, and when the action is long continued, an excitement is transmitted to the coledock duck, which which opens into the duodenum, from the liver & gall bladder, and causes these organs to secret a large quantity of bile, which is disgorged by the mouth, and the inference drawn, as comonaly is, that there is an undue quantity of bile in the stomach.

Hiram Rutherford's notes at Jefferson Medical College. *Courtesy Austin Rutherford.*

The operation of Calomel is confined in most cases to the Duodenum; this is manifested by the sickness which is felt soon after taking a dose; of consequence the excitement extends up the ductus Coleauches to the liver & gall-bladder, an increased secretion is the effect, so that to to give Calomel in health, it will produce a bilious disposition, the very disease it was intended to prevent.

Nov 9.   Lecture 2nd Urea.

The urine contains two substances or principles, an acid, & an alkali; which of course stand in opposition to each other. The acid is called Lithic and it tinges the urine of a dark brown and leaves a brick-dust sediment deposited at the bottom of the pot. When it predominates, it forms stone, but they are soft and easily broken. The other is a phosphate which turns the urine of a light transparent colour, & forms the hard phosphates of lime stones, which are so hard to detatch from the bladder. These two principles when properly balanced, contribute to the healthy function of the bladder, but the predominance of one or another leads

Hiram Rutherford's notes at Jefferson Medical College. *Courtesy Austin Rutherford.*

to disease. The treatment in each case is directly opposite it must depend on the laws of Chemistry, for the acid apply an alkali such as the Magnesia Soda &c. for the other, acids are to be administered, such as the Nitric Sulpuric & muriatic. The misapplication of these remedies has the invaria effect of increasing the disease.

Albumen is never found in healthy urine nor in derangement of the bladder, but only in disease of the kidneys when their structure is altered. The patient is seyed with incontinence of urine, being obliged to rise and void it every ten minutes, and the bladder is so irritable that constant pain and anxiety is the consequence there does not appear any disorder of the kidneys but all the symptoms of stone is manifested in the bladder, but the sound finds nothing, and the physician is puzzled. Now take some of the urine which is always clear and bright, and hold it over a candle in a spoon till the heat arrives to 160 degrees, if there is albumen, it will coagulate and then may be safe inferred there is disease of the kidneys, which is often Hy dratids.

Hiram Rutherford's notes at Jefferson Medical College. *Courtesy Austin Rutherford.*

Dr. Rutherford's medical diploma. *Courtesy C. R. Rutherford.*

Dr. Rutherford's home, Oakland. *Photograph by Carol Buckler.*

Dr. Rutherford's office, Oakland. *Photograph by Carol Buckler.*

The Night Call on an Errand of Mercy, from Lucius H. Zeuch, *History of Medical Practice in Illinois*, Vol. I. *Courtesy Illinois State Medical Society.*

The Articles

The Articles

In 1877, recently retired from his medical practice, Dr. Rutherford began writing a series of recollections about Oakland and its first settlers. His essays were first published in the Oakland *Herald*, and in 1879 extracts from these essays were published in *The History of Coles County, Illinois*.[1] Files of the 1877 *Herald* have not survived, and though some of Dr. Rutherford's articles were reprinted in the Oakland *Messenger* in 1904 and 1905, those files are not extant either. Members of the Rutherford family and Mrs. Helen Parkes provided clippings of the articles, but it is not clear that all of his articles have been found.

All of the newspaper articles probably had titles when they first appeared in 1877, but some of these titles were omitted when they were reprinted in 1904 and 1905. Our ordering of the articles is of necessity arbitrary since we do not know Dr. Rutherford's intentions, nor the order in which they appeared in 1877. We place the stories about John Richman and Jonas Bragg at the end of the collection since they were not published during Dr. Rutherford's lifetime. Obvious scribal and typographical errors have been silently corrected, and occasional punctuation has been added for clarity.

The content of these articles is quite different from that of the personal, often emotion-charged letters. As Dr. Rutherford remarked in his essay "John Richman, A Typical Backwoods-

1. *The History of Coles County, Illinois*, pp. 443–56. This section of the county history was most likely written by Dr. Rutherford.

man," "looking backward, recalling a youthful epoch, the reminiscences of a past generation, is the pleasing task of old age," and he has fulfilled "the office and duty of history" with the writing of these essays.

In 1840 Dr. Rutherford had come to a part of Illinois where the prairie was virtually untouched. There were only a few settlers, in a village with no stores, no schools, and little religious activity. By 1877, when he began his historical sketches, Oakland had a dentist, five physicians, four attorneys, clothing and food stores, a school, a book and music store, drugstores, an undertaker, a photographer, churches, a newspaper, and a railroad. In less than forty years, the changes had been staggering, and Dr. Rutherford set out to describe Oakland and its people as he first knew them.

The articles are notable for their sense of time and place, for their humor, for their characterizations, and for the picture they give of an educated physician observing the people and events of a newly settled area. It is probable that Dr. Rutherford picked up most of his writing skills through his own reading. It is not now possible to re-create his entire library, for many volumes passed to relatives and friends after his death. However, we do know he brought to Illinois his copies of William Grimshaw's *History of England*; P. Horry's *The Life of Gen. Francis Marion*; Sir Humphry Davy's *Consolations in Travel*; and W. H. Ireland's *The Abbess, A Romance*. He also owned standard works, such as those by Byron, Cooper, and Homer, and he subscribed to such magazines as *The Atlantic Monthly*, *Gentleman's Magazine*, and *Scribner's*.

Dr. Rutherford described the personal strengths and weaknesses of ne'er-do-wells and solid citizens, always with affection and understanding. We believe that he consciously avoided discussing in public the intimate lives of his fellow citizens. Had he adopted a pseudonym, as did Dr. Henry Clay Lewis (Madison Tensas) in *Odd Leaves of a Louisiana Swamp Doctor*, he could have written at will about his patients, living and dead. But Dr. Rutherford obviously rejected that approach. When he wrote about personal matters, he was sensitive to the ethical and moral issues involved. We know, for instance, from Dr. Rutherford's letter to

John Bowman on October 25, 1847, that Mrs. Sargent took her own life. She had been ill with a fever, had been "carefully treated" by the doctor, and was improving, when her "mental faculties" gave way. She took arsenic and concealed taking it until it was too late for Dr. Rutherford to counteract the poison. That death was particularly difficult for him because Mrs. Sargent had been Lucinda's close friend. He wrote privately about this event in considerable detail, for he knew that it was unlikely that his brother-in-law would ever be in Oakland; but when he wrote about Mrs. Sargent in 1877, for an Oakland audience, he did not mention her suicide. Instead, he gave a moving account of a simple woman who had freed her slaves, and he reported on part of their conversation during her last hours:

> Thirty years have passed away, but it seems to us but as yesterday, that we saw her sitting by her great fire-place indulging in her pipe, with death waiting at her elbow; a picture of stoical calm, which we have never seen equalled within our three score years of time. Referring to this subject she said to us: "I did not know whether it was right or not to free those children, but their mother had done so much for me in my days of poverty, that I could not sell them as my husband and friends urged. It does me now in my last hours, a world of good and comfort that I brought them with me and did as I did." Thus in her simple direct nature she passed away, unaware probably of the everlasting brightness of the starry crown which she took with her.

Dr. Rutherford's praise was especially generous because he knew that many of his readers would remember that Mrs. Sargent took her own life.

His recollections were vivid, and many of his stories are in the best tradition of frontier humor: the tall tales of Billy Nokes; the mill fever of the settlers, even though the Embarras river (pronounced and often spelled Ambraw) was totally unsuited for mills; the exploding still; the dirty shifts of the two Ladd children; the elaborate names given to the male Ashmores; the Baptist minister given to strong drink. Dr. Rutherford, with his sense of the past and with his realistic details, transcends local history in these powerful chronicles, and tells us much more than the unique histories of a few people of the West in the 1840s.

Until now, the only essay of Dr. Rutherford's known to a wide audience has been "A Typical Backwoodsman," an account of the old frontiersman John Richman, which appeared, after the doctor's death, in the *Transactions of the Illinois State Historical Society* (1907) and was then reprinted in a 1910 history of Douglas County. The essay contains an amusing account of the doctor's minor surgery on the old hunter and Lucinda's involvement in repeating a "pow-wow formula," commanding the blood to stop flowing. Dr. Rutherford shows remarkable psychological understanding and skill in handling his patient by allowing old Richman to retain his belief in witchcraft, while successfully using his own scientific methods. When the old frontiersman's incantation did not work, Dr. Rutherford wrote, "I did what I should have done at first, put on another and tighter bandage. But Mr. Richman was satisfied, nevertheless, that the 'words' had done the business."[2] Dr. Rutherford had not studied psychology at Jefferson Medical College, but he was evidently a master at applied psychology.

Dr. Rutherford's entire account of "A Typical Backwoodsman" is a masterful piece of writing, deservedly well known and remembered. Sometime in the 1930s, Mark Van Doren, while visiting his brother in Tuscola, Illinois, came across the reprint of the story of John Richman and his pet deer and was fascinated by it. As Van Doren remarked in his *Autobiography*, the events in the story "seemed mythical." "History in them for once was poetry, as if an artist had controlled events."[3] Later a friend told Van Doren the same story, saying it had happened on the Wisconsin frontier. Van Doren concluded that the story of Richman's search for the deer was legend, not history. Dr. Rutherford's daughter, Anna, was incensed by Van Doren's doubts, saying that she knew the Richman family, and that the events had happened just as her father wrote them. Mark Van Doren's long

2. Dr. Rutherford's spelling had improved. In the 1840s he consistently misspelled *business*.

3. Mark Van Doren, *The Autobiography of Mark Van Doren*, p. 238.

narrative poem, *The Mayfield Deer*, inspired by Dr. Rutherford's article, is most effective when it stays close to the source.

Van Doren's poem and the long comments about Dr. Rutherford's story in Van Doren's *Autobiography* called attention to the doctor, but still his other sketches remained unknown. Many of the sketches are just as evocative as the story about Richman. Dr. Rutherford's stories about ministers are particularly revealing and are often written with a wry humor which might have distressed some readers when they came across the stories in the Oakland newspaper in 1877. Some Baptists could have been disconcerted to read about a Baptist minister who drank too much; some Methodists might have been upset by Dr. Rutherford's account of the man "Bragg by name and brag by nature," but that story never appeared at all, perhaps because of the religious comments. This marvelous story, with its mock-heroic beginning, its strong characterization of the braggart frontiersman, and his difficulties with the Methodists, ends this section. In this collection of essays, we see Dr. Rutherford as a shrewd observer of people and events around him. At times he merely observed and reported, at other times—in the account of the "mud sill" Lord E. Archer, for example—he probed psychological states. Like Thoreau in Concord, Dr. Rutherford traveled much in Oakland. We can only lament that he did not write more.

1.

At the Centennial celebration of Independence held at Charleston, last year, his Honor, Judge Adams,[1] in accordance with previous arrangements, produced an historical sketch of the early settlements in Coles county; and necessarily therewith more or less reference to some of its earliest pioneers. It is needless to say that the people of Coles felt then and always will feel grate-

1. Judge William E. Adams was County Judge in Coles County and Secretary of the Coles County Old Settlers' Society.

ful to the judge, for his careful and interesting effort in anti-quarian research. But with regret they realized the fact, that a few columns of a newspaper contained the whole address. If we recollect aright Oakland and vicinity was barely mentioned by Judge Adams, and that portion of the then Coles county—Douglas county—was left entirely out. We presume that when the judge wrote up that epitomised history, he must have kept by him a pneumatic condenser, or probably a hay press to keep his work in bounds. Laying aside for the present the judge's condenser, we have thought to ourselves that even if Oakland never was a famous city, and never had any "poor wise men" in it, yet there might be something about it, and its neighborhood which, buried under the weight of nearly half a century, the readers of the HERALD today might wish to know, and knowing might possibly preserve for another fifty years.[2] To meet this imaginary want we propose in this and the following papers by the help of the few remaining old settlers, men and women, and our more recent recollections, to furnish a few items, local, per-sonal and otherwise, mixed and compounded with a few obser-vations (by the way of improvements) which, we will scatter about as we proceed along this highway of our pioneer history.

Captain Samuel Ashmore is admitted to have been the first settler in this neighborhood. Accompanied by his grown sons—Claybourne, who was then married, and George W. and Madi-son who were single men—he pitched his tent on what was long after known as the Laughlin farm, now owned by Mr. Andrew Gwinn and the heirs of Snoden Sargent. This was in the year 1829. In raising his house he had the assistance of John Rich-man[3] and his sons, who had about the same time settled on the head waters of the Embarras, twelve miles to the north west. At that time Paris and Grandview were the nearest settlements to him, though it is said that a solitary family then lived on Greasy creek, but if so their name and history are to us unknown. Other families may have come into the wilderness this year, one we think was by the name of Lamb, and perhaps another by the

2. Dr. Rutherford owned an interest in the Oakland *Herald*.
3. See art. 11 for an account of John Richman.

name of Thornsbreu, but they were birds of passage, wanderers or tramps and made no abiding place. It is not our purpose to magnify the labors or hardships of a first settler. It is true that the wild wilderness was before Mr. Ashmore, and the Indians were and continued to remain there for several years, but those trials had been underwent by others before him and by a multitude since his day. As a frontier man, his training, habits and education eminently fitted him for the work. Large of frame, strong in body and with a determined will; like Ajax he only asked for day light and fair play. Our excuse for an extended notice of him and his family lies in the fact that the romance of a country ever has and ever will attach to its first inhabitants. Of his family history we know nothing, almost absolutely nothing. From his surviving children and the descendents of his twelve sons and daughters, we could not even learn the name of his father or the place of his birth. Following the practice of scientific men—when all else fails—to read the past by the present, as the geologist reads the drift and the rocks, and the philologist, old and forgotten languages, we offer the following as a reconstruction of his family history; Ashmore, it will readily be seen, is a compound name; first, from the Angle Saxon Asc(ash) stiff, sturdy, a tree; second, More is a celtic or Irish word, and means great, large, powerful, etc. His fore-fathers, we judge, lived in the north of Ireland, and probably were comprised in the great Scotch-Irish emigration, which previous to the revolutionary war, settled so extensively in Pennsylvania, Virginia and other southern states. It is probable that Captain Ashmore was born in South Carolina or Georgia, but we first know of him living on Duck river in Tennessee. Here he had the honor of serving as a commissioned officer under General Jackson, was out in the Creek Indian campaigns, and fought at the battle of New Orleans. It is needless to repeat that his opinion of his great commander bordered on reverence, and was fondly cherished by him to the day of his death. Resolving to leave Tennessee, whose chattel slavery he thoroughly detested, with his brothers William, James and Amos and all their families, he came to the Wabash country; here he soon fell into the chronic frontier style of life, common today as it was then. First to make an improvement and next get too hot for a sale, and that is made, go to chopping again upon another claim. If it be true that a rolling stone gathers no moss, it is apparent that the tramp farmer is a failure. By the help of his sons he opened a farm near Darwin, cleared off one hundred acres of bottom timber, built a two story house, several stables and out houses and after that he sold the whole caboodle to his son-in-law for $600, in order to get to the Ambraw country. It is scarcely necessary to say that Mr. Ashmore never became a rich man.

Having succeeded in selling his first location to Mr. Laughlin, Mr. Ashmore moved down to Hoge's branch, where most of his sons and sons-in-law had by this time settled. He commenced work on what is now known as the Barbour farm. Here after filling the office of justice of the peace, he died in 1838, aged as his tomb stone states sixty years.

One of the great difficulties of a biography is to sketch the character of a man whom the author has never seen. It is a still greater difficulty in the presence of his surviving children, and his descendents—"numerous as the sands of the sea"— to do that work faithfully, especially when all you can say of him is not praise. Like the rough frontiersman that he was his hand was ready, if struck, he returned the blow with interest and effect like a good son of the church militant; a strong friend and hospitable; a bitter enemy and vindictive. Probably he talked too much, a weakness common to the times when it was thought necessary for every man to give an opinion, whether he had a reason for it or not. Then again chimney corner jurisprudence was a fruitful subject for discussion; we don't know that in our own times the habit is any better than it was then. Mr. Ashmore had hot blood and in behalf of what he supposed was his "rights," spared neither himsef nor others.

"What was his disposition?" we inquired of his venerable and respected daughter-in-law.

"Well, sir, he was a very fractious man—when he got angry."

To show that he had a fountain of humor in him, it is related that driving cattle once in Tennessee, in a terribly muddy road, he met a broad cloth snob (broad cloth was scarce then) who in disregard of drover courtesies forced his horse into the midst of the herd, producing considerable confusion. In a moment Ashmore comprehended his man and riding up to meet him greeted him as an old friend, "Why, how are you!" held out his hand and grasping that of the snob's with an iron grip, he put spurs to his horse and dragged the fellow off his saddle into the mud.

2.

Mr. Eli Sargent of Piketon, Ohio, came the next year (1830), and located on the tract adjoining Mr. Ashmore, to the west. He was a man of wealth and enterprise, and entered several hundred acres. He too brought with him his sons and daughters. The latter made the journey on horseback, and had a gay old time riding through the wilderness. The world was not so wide then as it is now, and he and Mr. Ashmore soon discovered an incompatibility of temperament, which the narrow bounds of the country aggravated exceedingly. Mr. James Redden, in this same year located a mile west of Mr. Sargent. He built the first horse mill in the country, a grand institution by the way. His land still remains in the name of Redden, owned by Josephus, a grand son, and Stephen, his youngest boy; the latter a gay old boy now to be sure, but an evidence of the "survival of the fittest" and the general fitness of things.

Returning to Mr. Sargent we find him busy enough opening his farm and keeping even with his belligerent neighbor, a matter of habit on both sides perhaps—not dead in the world yet, but just about as sensible as a last year's birds nest. Health, the greatest blessing in life, was not for Mr. Sargent; seated leaning over a table, he passed weary days and nights, whilst the water gathered in his chest, higher and higher and his breath became shorter and shorter. Mr. Ashmore, so long a stranger to his house, called to see him, his heart softened at the sight and to his honor and manhood, be it said, tendered his sympathy, asked his pardon for the past and as a token of his faith and reconciliation, begged of him his hand. Mr. Sargent died in 1834. Of his family there still survives his daughter Mrs. Gwinn, and his step-daughter Mrs. Sargent, of this village, who have the honor, we believe, to be the only remains with us of the emigration of 1830. After Mr. Sargent's death his widow bought the Samuel Hoge farm and with her son John L. Berry and her daughter Rachel, made her home there, where she died in April, 1847, in her sixtieth year. Our recollection of this lady, is that of a high-spirited and dignified woman. Afflicted with asthma, she was an inveterate smoker of course, but possessed uncommon business capacity. Mounted on "Old Ned" in rain or sunshine, day or night, she attended all calls upon her professional services, and in this particular alone was an exceedingly useful person. What she loved, however, was probably more a matter of instinct than of calculation. Ned was a favorite; a large, brown pacing horse, which she had reared from a colt. Within the thirty years of his life he had carried her everywhere that she went; three times from the Ambraw to the Sciota;[1] he survived his mistress a year and has gone where the good horses go. Reared in Kentucky, Mrs. Berry had been left a widow with poverty and several young children for an inheritance. Her effects then consisted of twenty acres of ground, her horse Ned, a slave woman and her children. Sickness came, bread became scarce and the wolf looked in at the door. The slave woman and the horse did the farming, and Mrs. S. once stated to us that had it not have been for the woman and the horse, she would have come to absolute want. When she married Mr. Sargent, (who was a rich man) she removed with him to Ohio, taking Ned and two of the five children of the colored woman. To her she left the land, who after a trial of eighteen months, left it and went as a cook to a hotel in Louisville. Here she died and Mrs. Sargent had her other three children sent to Ohio, and ultimately brought them all to this country. Her most judicious advisers, including her husband had urged her to sell them to put them in her pocket, etc., and showed her the "black laws" of Illinois, and all the difficulties of the situation. But no, the memory of that woman and horse toiling in the sun, to raise bread for her and her children when she lay sick and prostrate, was not to be overcome. Worldly woman as she was, she pos-

1. The Scioto is a river in south central Ohio.

sessed a determined will and she decided never to sell them—as she expressed it to us "while my head was hot." Mrs. Sargent was a woman of limited education and knew nothing about the abstract doctrine of human rights. She had never heard of Clarkson or Wilberforce.[2] She was a Baptist, and neither knew nor cared perhaps, for Wesley's opinion on the "sum of all villainies," and of abolitionism, she concurred in the then common opinion, that its advocates were thieves of a hideous character. What was it that caused her to withstand the pressure of interest, was it gratitude or was it instinct, or was it both? Thirty years have passed away, but it seems to us but as yesterday, that we saw her sitting by her great fire-place indulging in her pipe, with death waiting at her elbow; a picture of stoical calm, which we have never seen equalled within our three score years of time. Referring to this subject she said to us: "I did not know whether it was right or not to free those children, but their mother had done so much for me in my days of poverty, that I could not sell them as my husband and friends urged. It does me now in my last hours, a world of good and comfort that I brought them with me and did as I did." Thus in her simple direct nature she passed away, unaware probably of the everlasting brightness of the starry crown which she took with her.

In 1831, Mr. Laughlin and the Pembertons, came from West Virginia. Mr. L. moved to Iowa, and died there. Mr. Pemberton was not healthy, and lived but a few years. His widow continued with us till 1854, and lies buried in the upper grave-yard. She was remarkable for three things, her candor, her good cooking and her genuine hospitality. Her son, Henry A. Pemberton, still lives on the old place, and "Uncle Jack," as the children call him, continues with us in the village, a well preserved specimen of the olden time. Not deeming it proper to sketch the living in our chronicle of character, we yet forbear; Uncle Jack's time has not yet come.

Recurring to the Ashmore family, we find that Samuel Hoge, a son-in-law, this year entered the Berry farm and probably

2. Thomas Clarkson (1760–1846) and William Wilberforce (1759–1833) were leaders in the movement to abolish the British slave trade.

settled on it at once. About the same time Mr. Ashmore's sons, James and Hezekiah, came to this country; the latter entered the land which our neighbor D. W. Powers has occupied for the last forty years. On this place our present sheriff was born. During all these years and for years thereafter, there was a constant stream of transient emigrants; men contented in but one particular, and that was when they were on the move going from place to place. Like the grasshopper, they would stop and feed for a while, getting credit wherever they could, giving promises in abundance, then lighting out for parts unknown between two days. Such no doubt, are the fire flies of the frontier to-day, who light up the borders of the great American desert.

3.

The land upon which the now village of Oakland is built, was entered by David McCord, in 1834. He built upon it a little log cabin of about 14 × 16 opposite our residence where our stock well stands. It happened that this, the first house built on these lands did in the course of time fall into our hands. We purchased the lot of John Davis, who then lived in a larger and better log house on the site of our before-mentioned residence. Reserving Mr. Davis[1] for a future notice, we would remark of the little log cabin, that having had no present use for it, and unaware of the interest or romance of its origin, we sold this "relic" for the paltry sum of five dollars, and have forgotten to whom; only, that it was wanted for a stable. Mr. McCord was bought out by Mr. Josiah Black, a son-in-law of Mr. Ashmore, the same or early the next year, who built a double log house on what is now Pike street; partly covered at present by the residence of his son, Jas. S. Black. The next year, 1835, was famous for its town site speculations in Illinois, and Mr. Gideon M. Ashmore, having taken the "fever," bought of Mr. Black a small tract—sixteen or eighteen acres off of the s. e. s. e., of sec. 13, T.14, R.10 upon which he proceeded to lay out a town site. Mr. Canterberry, an attorney-at-law and county surveyor, came up

1. See art. 5.

from Charleston, and after making due measurements, pegged it down and plotted and recorded the work so done in A. No. 1 style. This plat embraced the south side of the village from the middle of the public square. Sales being encouraging, Mr. Ashmore soon afterwards purchased an additional tract and completed his town site on the north. Matt, as he was called for short, was a speculator by nature, had much good gas in him and believed in names, high-sounding ones of course; but from the resources of his very limited education, he drew liberal draughts upon uncommon or little-used words, which words he made still more remarkable by his unheard of pronunciation. On this subject of names we once heard him offer a plea. His father, it appears, possessed the name of Samuel, a single simple name, in accordance with the puritanic tastes of our ancestors of a hundred years ago. He called his first son James, but adopting the "rolling stone" or rovers life, he soon became sensible that he was not to be a child of fortune. Strongly attached to his children, he gave them all he could give them, instead of money and lands, great tremendous names, such as Hezekiah Jefferson, Samuel Claybourne, George Washington, Gideon Madison, Omar and finally General Jackson. It is sad to relate that his poor girls had to put up with simple common, every day names. Matt, a full sketch of whose character we reserve for a future occasion,[2] went the way of his father, only more so. He not only named his children (his boys, we mean) after the great ones of this world, but every thing he possessed from a dog up, had a heavy or patriotic title tagged to it. After mature study, he called his new paper town "Independence" and in the same spirit, he afterwards laid out the town of "Liberty," two miles north of Ashmore, but "Virtue" still remains to be platted. The name Independence was in many respects objectionable, it was too long, too many syllables, and malice and spite soon found for it a nick name in "Pinhook," which name stuck like a burr, and for a long time it was generally known by that alias. Even yet we occasionally hear this name from ill-bred or simple minded

---

2. We have been unable to locate this article on Matt Ashmore, which undoubtedly dealt, in part, with Mr. Ashmore's role in the Matson Slave Trial.

people. In 1851 the name was changed by act of the legislature to Oakland, the name which the post office had always borne.

Mr. James Ashmore, known as "Squier Jim," is said to have put up the first buildings—all of logs. One was the old tavern which stood where the Oakland house now stands; another was on the corner occupied by Frank Coffin's store room, and a third, the most famous was a business house where Cash's brick store now stands. Here "Squier Jim" opened his law office, and John Wesley Sanders, a hunchback man, sold groceries, feed, etc., but whiskey more than all else. We will not stop just now to enlarge on the whiskey traffic then; like the looking glass it always reflects a true image, and he who would see a picture of what it was here thirty or forty years ago, can now find it anywhere along the frontier, or in the mining districts. How long law and whiskey held together, we are not informed. The idea then attached to the term "business," was to gather up a few "traps" or notions, make a start and sell out—the successor adding a few to the stock and "lumping it off" upon the first opportunity. If he got cash, which was seldom the case, he sold "dog cheap"; if on credit, the price was high; he discounted the note heavily or traded it for what he could get as soon as possible. Hence arose the story of the man who traded his goods for a dog, and then to close the concern, killed the dog. Sanders was a fair sort of a man, and had a reputation for gallant and chivalrous bearing. After wandering about for a number of years, he returned to this country and laid out "Warrenton," on Donica point. In the meantime "Squier Jim," did more for the town than Matt himself, built a frame storehouse on the corner now occupied by D. W. Mitchell. In this house John McClellan sold dry goods and general assortments in 1836. In '38 or '39, Jonas Trembly, a merchant of Georgetown, opened up a stock of goods in the log grocery and law office. These men, McClellan and Trembly, had no trouble in selling their goods, the difficulty lay in collecting. Nearly every family had a loom and provided their own woolen goods, jeans and flannels, but cotton goods had to be bought. Domestic sold at twenty cents per yard, and the luxuries of sugar, tea and coffee, much the same price as now. The means of payment were extremely limited. Corn, the great staple of the country, could not be sold for money, it traded at ten cents per bushel. A four year old steer would bring ten dollars, and cows of first quality sold at the same price. They were bought up for the Wisconsin market. Hogs were then as they are now the great live stock staple of the country, and sold from four dollars down to one per hundred net. For butchered beef, the little sold, rated at two and three cents per pound.

The first blacksmith shop was opened at the north-east corner of the public square under a walnut tree, by a man named Maxey. Next to him in the same line, came Dick Hawkins; his shop stood where Tom Hodge's house is and his place of residence was on the lots where Dr. Peak now lives. Hawkins rented his shop and tools to John Hall, and moved to the Scattering Fork. Hall hammered away more or less for a couple of years, and then helped Mr. Trembly to take a drove of cows north. Hawkins returned after a while, and after him came the late David McConkey. Of carpenters there was none; every man was his own boss workman, and Mr. Jack-of-all-trades was a much more common and important gentleman than he is now.

Doctor Sterling Combs was the first physician. He located in 1836. Belonging to a consumptive race, he was short lived. A pretender named Montague, set up the next year, but a large portion of the practise was done by the Conduitts of Paris. Montague fizzled out and Dr. Wm. Patton started in the race for public favor, in 1838. Dr. P. made it a success, though a man with very little medical or other education. He remained till 1847, and then took to wandering; removed to Ohio, thence to Quincy, Ill., and died in Iowa, possessed of a considerable amount of this world's goods. He was distinguished for his lameness, his deafness and his inability to utter a word when he was angry. He filled the office of postmaster for many years. One of the Conduitt brothers (Wellington), located at the same time Dr. Patton did, but did not stay. He, like Combs, fell a victim to consumption. James and Alonzo Conduitt continued at Paris, and practiced much all over this country. We have heard James state that they rode from Bruitts creek, to the Brushy Fork of the Ambraw and that it took three days to make the circuit. Lastly our own self set up our tin sign in the last days of 1840.

The prairies were then without an inhabitant, save the deer and the wild wolf. Dr. Bacon for years did all the practice on the Okaw timber. He lived near Bourbon, Dr. Willard was a Grandview, and Charleston, Paris, Georgetown and Urbana, were the next nearest points where physicians were located, and upon whom the settlers depended in the frequent malarial sickness of those days.

4.

As a sequel to the mercantile subject which mainly occupied our last paper, we beg to add a few paragraphs as to the mechanics of Oakland—the builders of the business and other houses erected during the period embraced in No. 8.[1] Robert Bell was one of the first carpenters who came to this part of Illinois. He built and owned the house where H. D. Williams resides, and lived there a number of years. He built the house in which Dr. Peak lives and many other structures of less note. As a joiner he was superior to any workman we have ever known, and much of his work which remains will, we think, bear out our estimate. In those days the finishing lumber a carpenter had to work with, was undressed poplar. No planing mills or sash factories then. Everything needed in the construction of a house, including flooring, moulding, etc., had to be worked out by hand. House frames were generally of hewed material with the corner post rabbited.[2] The price of lumber at the time we refer to, was usually about $10 per M, but had to be hauled from the Wabash country. A carpenter's wages were a dollar to a dollar and a quarter per day, and common labor about half that price, yet it cost more to put up a house then than it does now. At an early day our venerable friend Andrew Gwinn, with the help of "Billy Nokes," supplied our market by whipsaw, at the rate of four dollars per hundred. Two men could saw two hundred feet per day. Mr. Gwinn and Nokes by this laborious process, manufactured a good many thousand feet. Mr. Bell removed to Newman, and

1. Dr. Rutherford is perhaps referring to art. 3 or art. 10.
2. *Rabbeting* is the grooving of boards or timbers before fitting them together.

is said to be residing at this time somewhere in Southern Illinois. John Barber came to this country in 1846. He happened to own some very good woodland west of town, and being a tolerably good workman, did more building for our citizens than any other person. He went to Iowa about twenty years ago.

It would not be fair to omit in our catalogue of mechanics Mr. Alpheus Jaques, the wagon maker, "Jake away off," as Nicols Curtis called him. He came here in '41, we believe, and was a connection by marriage with Barney Russel. If he is living to-day, we think it probable that he is the same boyish man that he was when we knew him here. His delight was a pair of little rat like ponies which he drove in style; going out of town or when he thought anyone was looking at him like the wind, and coming back as Dave McConkey described it, like "cats-a-fighting." If you wanted to raise a storm, just drop a hint disrespectful of the ponies, and if you wanted a favor, praise them and Jaques' heart would forthwith soften like wax. He made wagons and buggies out of old rails and most anything he could pick up. His skill with the draw-knife was remarkable, and the rapidity with which he turned off work was equally so. Within the conglomerate mass which is required to make a world, Jaques was a many sided crystal, a crystal whose colors and hues depended upon the quantity and the quality of the light which fell upon it.

Thirty or forty years ago, the mill business was a great favorite with the public, greater it seems to us than it is now. The possession of a horse mill was a mark of respectability; to own a saw or grist mill, was (as Mr. Jaques termed it) to be the "biggest toad in the puddle." The early settlers were on the look out for mill sites and although the Ambraw and its tributaries had nothing better than mud bottoms and low alluvial banks to offer, they discovered beautiful locations in abundance, and proceeded in pursuance of the statute laws to summon juries and condemn sites. As a dam three or four feet high would back water about as many miles on this sluggish stream quarrels and law suits were the order of the day, when the damage of back water was apprehended. At the horse-shoe bend near Bridgeport, where the river makes a circuit of three miles, and returns to within a quarter of its departure, people supposed that the owner of the "neck" had a "good thing in it." When the proprietor came to look at his land, the advantage spoken of was pointed out and much voluntary aid offered to forward the improvement. Before taking the fever, however, he leveled across the "neck" and found as he reported to us, that the channel was just one inch deeper above than it was below. Everybody in this vicinity had decided that the proper place for a mill was at that point on the river where it crossed the northwest corner of section twelve, and here Mr. Laughlin and others commenced operations. Mr. L. did not have much success, and let other people try their luck. When we first knew this mill it was run by Henry McCumbers—"Old Spalt," as he was called. Like his predecessors, he bestowed a great amount of labor upon this "folly," and got very small returns for it. Built upon the sand, when the floods came the mill sunk, or the bank washed away, or the engineering muskrat had bored a hole through the dam, or the wheel had become buried in drift and mud. With a perseverance worthy of a better fate, "Spalt" struggled on for a few years and then gave it up. Once more, a man by the name of Whitlock tried it, but quit exhausted [after a] year's struggle, having sawed one log. At last a friendly flood took away the abandoned frame, and the untroubled waters are now permitted "to glide slowly by, on their winding way to the sea." Mr. Chadd had a genius for mill interests, and built a mill just above the railroad crossing. The mud sills are still visible at low water, and a few large boulders which he used to weight down his dam with. Undershot turbine and reaction wheels were tried in vain, till a giant flood carried the thing away. David McConkey had worked night and day in his smith shop for years, till he had made considerable money. If he knew how to earn it, he failed to know how to keep it. Well enough would not do, he must be better. Taking the mill fever he lavished all he had on a site a little below Mr. Chadd's. It was the old, old story, the floods took the worthless concern away and he returned a broken man to his shop, and died in poverty. His wife ended her days in the asylum at Jacksonville, and his children are scattered to the four winds.

In the meantime the use of steam was slowly crawling into

favor. Clement and Clark in 1854, put up the first mill within the corporate limits. It was a grand institution in Oakland, and people went to see the engine work and to shudder when the steam blew off. A sash saw was attached to it and proved a great public benefit. The latter appurtenance was soon dispensed with, and although the concern has frequently changed hands, it grinds its grain to-day as well as ever, under the skillfull hands of the Zarley Brothers. The other mill known as the Smith mill is of modern date and was built by W. P. West. This man was what might be termed a fool for luck, and a spendthrift by nature. His father gave him a large farm at Culver's grove. Getting embarrassed he sold out, came down to this part of the country, and worried a while with the McConkey mill. He next got hold of the Frank Williams steam grist and saw mill close to the iron bridge. He succeeded in trading this worthless property to Thomas Kinney for a No. 1 farm; he commenced building the mill before referred to, at the same time he set up a grocery. About this time he succeeded in becoming guardian for the Wm. Franklin heirs for whom he drew pension money to the amount of eleven hundred dollars. His luck continuing good, his grocery burnt down, and he received $1,500, of insurance. His borrowed money began pressing upon him and he sold out to his partner, W. O. Smith, at a very good figure. If he had stopped here he would have had a good living remaining, but an old Shylock from Kansas, of the name of Foulke, succeeded in selling him a rattle trap mill in that place for about $5,000, which was really worth about that many cents. This last stroke finished him, cleaned him up, and it is said that he is still following up the mill business; but of course in a second hand way, enjoying under a mountain of debt the delusion of Tom Kinney, "that where he lost his means was the right place to find it again."

5.
Whiskey

This well known word is one of the very few which the Irish have added to the English language. It is unnecessary to comment upon its potency or prevalence in civilized or savage life throughout the world. It is certainly the king of artificial drinks. Our purpose in this paper is to tell of its ways and works in the early days of this village.

We have heretofore stated that the first business house was first occupied as a doggery.[1] This house as we have seen was next used for the sale of dry goods, and of course the law and whiskey business had to go into other quarters. Sometimes in one place and sometimes in another. In this connection we would remark that the veteran whiskey drinker of to-day will vainly sigh for the good old times when no government tax troubled the people, not even a license from any local authority, interposed in the enjoyment of either whiskey or tobacco. Ten cents per quart left a great margin for the vendor, and the happy consumer had the satisfaction of knowing as he swallowed the beverage, that it was the pure corn juice or honest "bald-face" that assuaged his burning thirst. Oil of vitriol or strychnine whiskey was then unknown.

It was, we believe, in 1840 (we hope the reader will excuse our mistaken dates) that Joshua Davis, a heavy set, sore-eyed man came to Independence. He had with him his son-in-law, Jim Ladd, and his sons Merriman, Nat, Uriah and Welch. This strong force of men should have done something in the way of building up the town. But to tell the truth about it they were a desperately lazy set, and as a matter of course were shockingly dirty. As a "specimen brick" in this latter particular we will state that Mrs. Ladd had two children of five and seven years—a girl and boy if we remember rightly. Their dress consisted of but one garment made like a shirt or slip, which reached to their bare knees. This convenient covering did duty day and night, and certainly never saw the inside of a wash tub for one summer season. By long and judicious usage the fronts and backs of these dresses had become very dark, thickened and glazed with dirt and grease, whilst the sides were of a primitive yellow and comparatively mobile, resembling as a whole the shell of a turtle in a striking degree.

1. A cheap saloon.

Most of men live by their wits but the Davises struck a medium and lived partly by labor. By a moderate use of the strong muscular power which nature had given them, they commenced building a doggery on the corner where the bank now stands. The logs for this building were cut on congress land, and were first squared and then whipsawed into plank of three inches in thickness. These were set on edge and joined at the corners, house log fashion. This house which now does duty as a dwelling a mile west of town, was opened for business near the close of the year; Mr. Daniel Swall furnished the capital which consisted of a barrel of whiskey and a few rolls of domestic tobacco. The two dry goods houses had by this time fizzeled out and Messrs. Davis & Swall, like Lot of old, had all the plain of the Ambraw before them.

The habit of country people coming to town on Saturday was as common then as it is now, and in this connection we had noticed that they immediately disappeared from the streets and would as a rule be seen no more that day. Passing by the doggery on one of these days, we heard issuing from it a loud continuous noise, and having a curiosity to see western life in all its phases, we stepped in to take a look at the congregation. Nobody was drinking just then. All were talking or speaking at the top of their voices, gesticulating wildly, and nobody appeared to be listening. Dodging around behind the stove, we took a seat by Lindly Ashmore and Lyman Keyes, who were just then disposing of a piece of dried beef. From this safe position we took observations on these groups before us, of which the reader will permit us to sketch one. Near us stood an undersized man in blue jeans and a wolf skin cap, engaged with a large blear-eyed, big-nosed individual, wearing a white hat. The large man had button holed his auditor; that is, he had grasped him firmly by both collars which rendered retreat impossible. The small man was not a good listener, his attention was careless and every half minute he broke into a line or two of some doggerel ditty that appeared to float about in his mind. From this state of oblivion he was recalled by a tap of his companion's great fist on his breast, and "now Jim I'll jist tell you what sort of a man I am!" Jim was aroused by the rudeness perhaps and inquired sharply,

"Ain't your name Old Yaller?" "Yes, Mr. Hunt," and the large man raised his fist and waved his great red nose. "Yes, people call me Ole Yaller, you know that that isn't my real name, but then people call me so. A nick-name is just as good as any, it don't make any difference in a name. I'll tell ye what Jim, I brought some yaller boys with me to this country, but I hain't got any now. I paid four hundred dollars in gold for the place I live on, and that's the way I got the name of Ole Yaller. You're a Whig and I'm a Democrat, but that don't make any difference either between us; I believe in doin' what is right and honest, and I try and do that way myself, though some of my neighbors who belong to the church, don't tell the truth always, but then that's their business. I'm from ole Virginny, and I believe what's right is right; that's me, that's jist the sort of a man I am—that's Ole Yaller!"

Of the men who wasted their substance and their lives around Davis & Swall's dead fall, many of them were good estimable people in very many respects. Their thirst for liquor was by far their greatest fault. "Old Yaller" was a very kind, good man at home; so was John B. Dougherty, who carried to his grave the great wen on the side of his face. Lyman Keyes went to the Mexican War and left his bones at Chapultepec. Lindly Ashmore was a quiet peaceable person, and excelled in honor and honesty as we thought, all other men. We happened one day to pass some men sitting under the shade of a tree near Hall's smith shop, who were engaged in the then heated subject of politics. Ashmore, carrying as usual a pretty heavy load, sat with his eyes half shut and said nothing till a pause occurred in the conversation, when he remarked by way of interjection probably that the Whig party now was just the same as the Tories were in the revolution. At this Reuben Dannals, a man of seventy-five, sprang to his feet greatly excited. "Mr. Ashmore, you have insulted me, you have called me a Tory; you knew I was a Whig and you have called me a Tory. I am an old man and cannot help myself; I will not speak another word to you!" "Hold on Uncle Dannals, hold on," said Lindly, getting wide awake, "I ax yer pardon, that was all wrong, what I said was all wrong. I take it all back inter me, and I ax yer pardon." Wm. L. Ashmore never quit his drinking habits. Exposure brought on pleurisy; as the typhoid symptoms increased his mind wandered, and his hands picked the clothes, and hunted for jugs, and other drinking ware, and so passed away a man upon whose like this generation will probably never cast its eyes.

Times were hard and people had no money. It took money to buy whiskey and Davis & Swall resolved to start a distillery and make their own liquor. They put up a rough log building, covered with clap boards and weighted down with poles; and getting some mash tubs, by the aid of the horse mills around, they made a start on their new departure. When the first run was ready, men collected around the building; some with jugs and some without jugs, waiting for a free drink of the first run in accordance with old time custom. The elder Davis with candle in hand had visited the dark corner where the barrel stood to secure the precious beverage. Two or three times he had visited it and reported good news—the run was doing "beautifully" as he said, and the barrel was pretty well filled. Dan Swalls who was the most awkward blundering man we ever knew, became excited, snatched up the candle and started for the barrel. In his eagerness he held the candle too close, the spirits ignited, and the barrel exploded with a great noise, filling the house with steam and smoke. Soon after Jo. Stears who had a sore heel came limping by barefoot, and Squire Pemberton inquired of him "What's the matter down there Jo?" "Matter enough! the whole thing's blow'd to hell," and with a countenance expressive of unutterable disgust, Jo limped on ahead towards home.

The Davis family did not escape the penalties which nature has ordained against those who taste, touch and handle the unclean thing. After running their distillery a short time, they suspended and finally moved away, taking with them Mr. Ladd and his interesting family.

6.

Mud Sills

Many years ago when the slavery question was at its height, Senator Hammond, of South Carolina, in a political discourse before the U.S. Senate, held the opinion that civilized society like a culvert or a bridge, necessarily rested on a mud sill substructure, and in this subject or classification he included all laboring people.[1] Without presuming to criticise the senator's dogma which was well abused at the time, we deem it best in this paper, after adopting his nomenclature, to restrict our classification to those only, whose lives and habits in an eminent degree were of the earth earthy, anti-types of Sodom and specimen Turks. All communities are supposed to be blessed more or less by people of this character, and new countries or settlements therein usually have a Benjamin's portion of them. Our section of country had its foul mouthed, filthy people and possibly may have some yet, but we are dealing with the past and with those who have passed away, deeming it a true maxim that all de-merit as well as merit, has a right to be recorded.

Of Strawder Lamb, who so long lived with us, it might be said that the less written about him the better. That his power of nastiness in habit and conversation would be very difficult to describe, and then the mercian should, according to the practice of Gibbon, be wrapped in the folds of a learned or foreign language. Not being otherwise an interesting individual, we wash our hands and proceed to the next.[2]

Barney Russel was a native of Ohio. An immensely large, raw-boned man. He was very stoop shouldered, and on account of his extremely rough appearance, received from Lindly Ashmore the name of "Mountain Sprout." A name which he rather liked and which stuck to him whilst he remained in the country. Russel was a ready, quick-witted man, never at a loss for an an-

1. Senator James Henry Hammond (1807–1864), was elected to the Senate in 1857 and resigned his seat to return to South Carolina after Lincoln's election. His "mud sills" speech was delivered in the Senate on March 4, 1858.

2. Mercia was one of the Anglo-Saxon kingdoms and was located in what is now known as the Midlands. Mr. Lamb was probably a descendant of immigrants from the Midlands. Edward Gibbon (1737–1794), in *The History of the Decline and Fall of the Roman Empire*, did use Greek and Latin profusely in his notes. In the eighteenth and nineteenth centuries, these languages were often used to describe specific sexual practices. We assume that Dr. Rutherford was unable to reproduce Mr. Lamb's bawdy speech or comment on his sexual conduct in a family newspaper and therefore cited no examples at all.

swer, particularly when dirt and filth would suffice for a reply. He was a very good man to meet with at a horse mill; could help to kill time whilst waiting "turns" with anybody, and told his stories, such as they were, in good style. Like the late President Lincoln, his memory was stored with illustrations. Mr. Russel resided for a couple of years east of town, and there set up a cheese factory. In this line of business he was quite successful, his rennet cost him nothing, and our village ladies appreciated his cheese amazingly. It had, as they termed it, a "smarty state." Samuel Rains, another of these mud sills was more remarkable for his exceedingly repulsive appearance than for any other good or evil belonging to him. His mind was dark as Egypt, his vocabulary consisted of but few words, and some of these he pronounced in a way peculiar to himself. Owning a good farm, he never had five dollar's worth of goods in his house, and though ill to his family, provided enough to eat at least. He died in 1853, aged 68 years as his tomb stone in the upper grave yard, states. He invented the proverb "Let a man be a man, or a long-tailed rat."

Our last and best subject, as we think, was the late Lord E. Archer. Mr. Archer when we first knew him, was about fifty-five years of age. A large, muscular man and would weigh probably two hundred and fifty pounds. He claimed Vermont for his native state, but ran away from home when he was quite young. In excuse for this disgraceful act, he stated to us that his father was harsh and cruel to him. It might in this connection be said of him that his whole life was an illustration of the sentiment of Bulwer, "beware of that man who has been ill treated when a child."[3] In Ohio he set to work, and by industry gathered together considerable means, with which he emigrated to this country at an early day. He built the first house on Donica point and made an "improvement," which he soon succeeded in selling out to Tom Blair. He next located on the now John Dollar place, where he built a horse mill, all of which he rapidly disposed of and then bought the farm on which Mr. G. W. Hackett

3. Edward Bulwer, first Baron Lytton (1803–1873), was an English novelist much read in America in the nineteenth century. We have been unable to identify this quotation attributed to Bulwer.

now lives. In course of time he added to it the property on the Springfield road, where Mr. Gobert now resides, and at this latter place remained for a number of years. His power of consuming and carrying whiskey was simply wonderful. We have seen him drink tumblerful after tumblerful without causing prostration. He remarked to us once in reference to himself as a very curious fact, that whenever he drank sufficient to warm him all through and all over, he then had enough. For this purpose, it required, he said, just about a quart but if he happened to take the least bit over that measure, it was sure to fly to his head.

Selfishness with him was a leading characteristic. He never traded when he was drunk, and always bought his whiskey by the quart or gallon. In his trading practice, public opinion had no terrors for him if it stood in the way of gain. His motto was to make money, honestly if he could, but to make it any how. Hence those who traded or trafficked with him had to keep their "eye skinned." That he had any conscience, many people doubted. We happen to know better; he had. One day he sent us an urgent call, but before reaching his house we met another messenger under whip. Lord E. was bad, we could hear his lion like voice in anguish, a hundred yards from the house. We found him suffering with strangulated hernia. We had the good fortune to relieve him in a minute or two, and of course the intense pain ceased instantly. Mr. Archer rose up on the side of the bed and as we happened to stand in front of him, he placed his hands upon our cheeks and gently drew us nearer to him. As fast as his exhausted breath would allow him, he poured out a torrent of gratitude and affection. "Oh, doctor, you have saved my life; I always did love you; I always will love you, and I never will try to cheat you again." We made no answer, and probably misunderstanding our bewilderment, he immediately added with great energy, "Do you think I ever will try to cheat you again?" "No, no, certainly not, Mr. Archer," we hurridly replied, but as he gave us no farther explanation we are in the dark to this day, as to what transaction or incident he alluded.

We will ask the patience of our readers whilst we produce another "proof" in point. Mr. Archer's craving disposition caused him to work his boys to the verge of endurance. They were stunted, and grew up small bodied men, in striking contrast to his own towering form. Giving was not his forte. We never heard of him giving a cent to any civil or religious purpose. He gave nothing to his children and pocketed every dime that they earned. To provide themselves with pocket money for shows, etc., the boys stole his corn and sold it to movers, a clandestine operation likely to induce light fingered habits. One of these boys was married and lived as a tenant on his father's farm. Finding a pair of velveteen pants hanging at the store door of Burson & Elliott one day, he appropriated them, but failing to conceal them had to give up the "swag." The conditions of the "arrangement" was that he had to leave the country, and being without money he applied to his father. At that time Mr. Archer was sick, he had been suffering for several weeks with a catarrh in his head, and believing his end near at hand, had engaged Squire Pemberton to write his will. Having an unsettled account against the fugitive, we called on the old man a few days after the boy's flight, to see what was our prospects. We found Mr. Archer pillowed up in his rocking chair and he commenced at once to tell us of his trouble. He stated that when Burson & Elliott were in the house making a good deal of confusion, he had enquired of them what was the matter; they told him what it was, but he could not believe it, and he therefore called the boy up to him where he sat in the chair and asked him, "O——, did you steal the pants?" "Well, father I guess I took them." "Now," said Mr. Archer, "it had never come into my mind that I had ever raised a child to steal, and I felt then that I wanted to die. But the boy said he had to go, and had no money, and he wanted me to give him ten dollars. I told him to wait till morning, but he said he had to go that night, and Burson & Elliott put in and said he must go. So I gave him the ten dollars. Did I do right? I wanted to see you ever since, to ask you if I did right. If it wasn't right and I think it was not, I could not help it, I could not see him go out into the night and into the snow, without a cent of money." At this point the old man broke down, and placing his face in his hands he wept for some time. We sat by and saw the tears come through his fingers, and heard him pray in the intervals of his sobbing, that he might die. Words of sym-

[95]

pathy, like water, are a cheap commodity, but there are scenes and circumstances where they are useless. We know of nothing so sad and distressing as to hear an old man cry. At last he partially cleared up, wiping away his tears. "Oh, doctor, I know I did wrong to give him that ten dollars, but I could not help it. (Here he broke again.) But then I took for it his cow, his oat stack, three shoats and five acres of corn." Our tale is done. Notwithstanding his intemperate habits, his iron frame endured till far in his eighty-fourth year. He departed in September 1866, and lies buried in the upper grave yard, the oldest man probably who ever died in this part of the country.

7.
Romance and Reality

Amongst the various persons whom it has been our duty to notice in this veracious history, our readers will remember Billy Nokes—he who held the position of pitman, in the Gwinn whipsaw mill. Billy was a good humored, stoop shouldered, heavy set sort of a man; a man who had in him a large amount of muscular force; an amount so great in his own estimation, that he told some most extraordinary stories about it. Like the generality of romancers, Mr. Nokes was interested in himself more than in any body else, and hence his tales were invariably of a personal character. The first time we ever saw Mr. Nokes, he informed us that he was a native of Kentucky, and that in his younger days in that grand old state, he had made a sensation amongst his female friends. Although a snubnosed, big mouthed, coarse featured man, he had been compelled at a single term of the court at Louisville, to answer to twelve different suits for breach of promise. As a proof that he was a distinguished character people called him "Old bag o' shot," a name which he received as a reward for a story of his once carrying a sack containing a half bushel of shot on the streets of Louisville. Nokes said that the frost had just then came out of the ground, and that the weight was so great that the pavement bricks piled up about his feet and legs every step. This story grew in its retail till the shot amounted two bushels, and the displaced brick reached to his waist. We once met Mr. Nokes at Squire Ashmore's where he made a complaint of an assault and battery. His face was scratched, his lip fearfully swollen and one eye which was black as night, gave him a seriously comic appearance. The assaulter was a boy of eighteen, and Billy explained that the "pup" had taken him by surprise. The squire persuaded him, that it would not look well for a man who had carried two bushels of shot, to prosecute under the circumstances, and so Nokes in his good nature withdrew the complaint. Many years ago he moved to Iowa, and died there.

During the winter of 1830 and '31, two families camped on the west bank of the Ambraw, where the state road and the railroad now cross. That was a winter of deep snow, and when it melted the river rose higher than it has ever done since. The subsiding waters left a large log on the east bank near where Mr. Rollin's house now stands. One of these two families was that of Aaron Collins, who was the first settler on Greasy creek, and built the house in which his son-in-law Rees McAllister now lives. Mr. Mason, the head of the other family settled upon the land where he camped, now known as the Naphew farm. Mason did not hold the property very long and sold out to Wm. Chadd, a blacksmith, mill wright and jack-of-all-trades, who came from White river Indiana below Vincennes. He had considerable means and by the help of his three sons and seven daughters, he soon opened out a respectable improvement. "Old Shad," as people generally called him, was a little weasened, dried up man of sixty, with a large nose and a very full eye. His tongue, however, was his most remarkable feature. Loose at both ends, he astonished his neighbors by his volubility, and the Munchausen-like stories he told about himself and his wealth.[1] As to his resources he professed to hold a bushel or two of "cut money" which he had laid by for an emergency. Like most of the early settlers, he took the mill fever, and in addition to his smith shop got up a corn cracker. "That is a very fine mill," said Mr. Pemberton one day, "Could you grind wheat on it?" "Well, yes, I

1. Baron Munchausen (1720–1797) was notorious for his exaggerated stories.

could if I had a bolting cloth; in fact I told the boys the other day that we'd try it so I took a bushel of very clean, nice wheat and ground it. I then took the grist over to Mr. Redden's and bolted it. Well, sir, I had a hundred pound of flour and two and a half bushels of bran." The bare posts of that excellent mill stood for many a long day by the road side, a memorial of old times but now rotted and mouldered away, as though they had never been. Mr. C. next built a mill on the river as we have heretofore stated, but without profit. According to his mill experience in Indiana, as he stated it, this enterprise should have been a success, but it wasn't.

There was no bee-moth in the country then, and Mr. Chadd was a successful manager of bees. One day he came to town in a great hurry for a box or something to put a swarm into. This swarm he described as the largest he had ever seen—about the size of a barrel. What was curious about it he remarked was, that the gum it came out of was "a little bit of a thing not bigger than a nail keg." Everybody had some of "Old Shadd's" stories to tell and possibly (as in the case of Nokes) they may have suffered inflation in the repetition. Our relations with Mr. Chadd and his family were intimate, but for some reason he was reticent with us, and with one exception, never "let out" in our presence. That time he happened to speak on professional subjects; showed us his spring lancet and his "pullikin" for drawing teeth, and estimated his delivery of the latter at several barrels, and of the blood shed by the former, at the hogshead measure. In this connection he stated that he had once been applied to to tap a woman for dropsy. From this duty he had shrunk, had plead ignorance and other disqualifications, but as no physician was in reach he made an effort. Although the lady was a small woman, he drew from her one hundred and twenty gallons.

Mr. Chadd was possessed in a high degree with personal dignity. His children treated him with profound respect; he was no joker, and did not permit any body to joke him. Any insinuation as to the truth of his stories he promptly resented, for he told them in dead sober earnestness. Seated on a horse block one day, conversing with Moseley and Pemberton on the subject of music, he observed that the Jew's harp, if properly made was the best instrument known. That he had once made one for a boy, a good big one several feet long, as remarked. The bows of frame he made of tire iron and the tongue was an inch steel bar. "Why you could hear it three miles!" At this point Mr. P. stupidly inquired as to how the boy got it into his mouth. Chadd treated the query with contemptous silence, but afterwards remarked to Mr. Moseley, "Jack would like to say something smart if he knew how." The limits of this article forbid further details. A volume would scarce contain the incidents of Mr. Chadd's eventful life. Who has not heard of his duel before breakfast, when in an 18 foot square room securely locked, he and his antagonist armed with knives fought for eight hours ankle deep in blood? Who has not heard of his quarry blast on White river, which required the labor and teams of a hundred men six months to remove? Who has not heard of his snake story, of his fish story and of his perpetual motion saw mill? Mr. Chadd was gathered to his Fathers long ago, in the fullness of time and at a good old age. We never saw a man die with greater dignity; like the patriarch Jacob he set his house in order and bid his family an affectionate farewell. His children are dead or scattered, but two of them remain with us. Of these, his eldest daughter Mrs. Rollin inherits much of his character and talents—a well preserved relic of the olden time.

This is a skeptical age and produces no great men, probably for the reason that our modern school system, like a railroad track, is a dead straight ahead process. In Scott's Marmion the aged Douglas is made to moralize and lament

> "The decay
> Of human strength in modern day."

So we look in vain for a successor or even a good imitation of the great past. Who now bears the mantle of Nokes and Chadd? Alas for this generation!

8.

In the continuance of our chronicle we pass over to the clerical profession. The Presbyterians organized the first church; it dates back to 1831. It entered the field with a pretty strong force; being composed of heterogeneous elements it never prospered much. They built a small log church on the site of the upper graveyard, which was turned into a school house in after years. They next erected a frame building upon the public square, 24 × 40; but for lack of funds could not finish it. It never was seated except by slabs and loose plank, and had a floor of the same character. Its vicinity to the law and whiskey den, caused the pious to mourn; "familiarity breeds contempt," and its open doors afforded a shelter and convenient place for the drunken to sleep off the fumes of their debaucheries. This was not all the dishonorable purposes for which it was used by those drinking, carousing, Godless ruffians; it ceased to be used for divine service, and in 1844 the present church was erected. Samuel C. Ashmore was the contractor and Robert Bell the builder. Much like its predecessors, it never had a coat of paint, but has survived one roof. Mr. Bennett was one of their first preachers. He was a native of the city of Philadelphia, educated at Princeton, and was a man of considerable refinement. From eccentricity, from romance or from fancy, he cast behind him the refinements of civilization, and proclaimed the gospel of peace in the then wild wilderness of Illinois. His close, studious habits made him averse to noise, and being a bachelor, his habit was to select his board in a family in which there were no young children. The then common practice of taking all the children to church, tried his nerves terribly. The cry of a child whilst he was delivering his sermon was sure to upset him, and in this particular we have heard ladies express after long years the profound mortification they had felt under his embarrassments or reproofs, by which he drew the attention of the congregation upon them. Strange to say the quiet low voiced Mr. Bennett married his antipode in these particulars—a tall lively girl—a daughter of Amos Ashmore, who could out talk and out laugh any thing within ten miles of her. Her love and respect for Mr. B. never seemed to interfere with her animal spirits, but a change came over him; when two, three or four children had gathered about his feet he was another person; he could study his sermons better than ever, and preach right along in the stiffest kind of a squall. A Mr. Montgomery was another preacher of this denomination, but of whom we know nothing, and Mr. McDonald supplied the congregation occasionally, as well as Mr. Vennable.

The Cumberland Presbyterians organized in 1843, under the preaching of Rev. James Ashmore, of Vermillion county, a son of Amos and brother of Mrs. Bennett. He is, we believe, the only survivor of the old time church organizations. A man of great industry and untiring energy in his calling, now enjoying a green old age.

The Methodist church of Oakland was organized by Rev. Mr. Salsbury in 1856, but remained in a quiescent state till Mr. Arthur Bradshaw came on the circuit in 1858. He breathed the breath of life into the dry bones lying loose around him, and made it a strong and prosperous congregation. Like Mr. Ashmore, Mr. B. is now "in the sere and yellow leaf."

Reserving our Baptist friends and their great preacher, Mr. Newport, for our next, we occupy the balance of our paper with an incomplete sketch of Thomas Affleck. The name, according to Boswell, is a contraction of Auchinleck, the name of an extensive estate in the Lowlands of Scotland. He lived in Dumfries and emigrated, we believe, in 1832. Settled at Clinton, on the Wabash, and from thence to Mr. Ashmore's new town in 1836. His son-in-law, McClelland, as we have stated, was the first person to sell dry goods in this "neck of the wood." Mr. Affleck's wife, a very amiable woman, died in 1840, and the first time we ever saw "Uncle Tommy," he occupied his house on the north side of the square alone, having only his dog, Princher, and his cat, Tom, for companions.

In several respects Mr. A. was a remarkable man, perhaps the most so of any man who ever lived in the village. At the time of our first acquaintance he passed his time much in looking after his farm, digging ditches, and exercising on his violin; running over those pathetic and delightful airs which has given Scotland the prerogative in song. His rendering of "Roy's Wife of Aldivalloch," was such as none but a native Scot could equal. With his chin pressed down upon his fiddle, his large head and great staring eyes above, together with his powerful voice he repeated and practiced the music of his native land. His knowledge of natural philosophy and the chemistry of the arts was very considerable, but mechanics was his master study. This faculty in him was a controlling power. He had been a grocer in Dumfries but was then, when long out of practice, unequaled in his making up a package; more coffee or pepper would be put into a paper than any body else could. Then when the lightning like job was finished, the form of the package and the turns of the wrapping thread, would be absolutely artistic. We have heard Mr. Moseley state, that for practice he had frequently undone his packages, but never could properly restore them. He was something of a hunter. When he wanted a prairie chicken he put a yoke of cattle to his sleigh and drove for the glades southwest of town. Here the cattle would feed along whilst Mr. A. would sit and wait for a bird to rise. Sometimes two rose at once and he generally saved them both, a proof, to our mind, that no man can ever be a bird shooter who is destitute of mechanical genius. On this point Dr. Pease, an amateur phrenologist,[1] found his head, on measurement to be twenty-four inches in circumference—equal to a No. 9 hat—and his bump of mechanics the largest he had ever handled, but the development of concentrativeness was extremely small; which, if the science be true, might account for the fruitlessness of Mr. Affleck's "speculations," as we called them.

One of these was a mode of moving sandbars and deepening the outlet channel of rivers and harbors. This process, as he often described it to us, was very similar to the jetty system now used by Capt. Eads at the mouth of the Mississippi.[2] It consisted in first confining the water by means of ballast and piling on each side of the desired channel. This means he held would, of

1. Phrenologists believed that the shape and size of the human skull indicated mental faculties and characteristics. For an account of phrenology in nineteenth-century America, see Madeleine B. Stern, *Heads & Headlines*.

2. For an account of Captain Eads (1820–1887), see *Dictionary of American Biography* (1930), s.v. "Eads, James Buchanan."

itself, in time effect its purpose, but to hasten it on he next proceeded to drive in the channel, every eight or ten feet, iron piling. These piling consisted of two flat bars perforated with inch holes and joined at the points, but designed to be separated above by the distance of an inch or less. He next let down between the bars thus constructed, sections of boiler iron twenty or thirty feet long, to a point near the bottom, where it was secured by pins placed in the bars. Thus when the work was completed it somewhat resembled the lower board of a plank fence, and like it the water forced underneath was expected to tear out a channel. This in brief is an outline of his idea. He claimed that he had successfuly applied it on the Clyde, and in other harbors in Scotland, and had presented his project and claims to the board of Admiralty. Of Sir James Graham,[3] the then head of the board, he spoke with his characteristic bitterness, and being in lack of means he turned his back in disgust upon the old world, to find a home and a grave in Illinois. We know nothing of the history of the jetty system, who invented it, or when it was first applied, but our recollection is that it was about 1830, or before, that Mr. Affleck endeavored to engage public attention of Great Britain to his process of deepening harbor outlets. Another of his ideas was that of the mower, upon which he insisted, long before any were ever seen or heard of here, that the principles of the saw and finger bars were necessary to its success.

But the habit of strong drink was the evil genius of his later days—the older he became the worse—and when under its influence his temper and invective was peculiar and terrific. He thus went on drinking himself to death as fast as he could, hoping in his unhappiness, soon to be at rest by the side of his deceased wife. His son-in-law, Rev. A. O. Allen, persuaded him at last to go with him to his residence at Terre Haute, but not till the old man had first exacted a pledge of Mr. Moseley and other citizens, that they would see to the return of his body when the end should come. He did not stay long. He parted with the

3. Sir James Robert George Graham (1792–1861) was named first lord of the admiralty in 1830. See *Dictionary of National Biography*, (1890), s.v. "Graham, Sir James Robert."

world and its troubles on the 2nd of June, 1852, aged 67 years; and Mr. Moseley and the citizens of Oakland, fulfilled their pledge and laid him by the side of the wife of his youth.

For information and data connected with these papers we lately visited the old grave yard. We made a considerable search before we found the resting place of Mr. Affleck. The slab which marks it had fallen down on the sunken grave and the weeds and grass were rank over it and about it. We had no implement with us to adjust the wrecked sepulchre, but we felt that we could not leave his memorial upon the ground, and so with considerable effort we raised and propped the slab with some decaying wood; promising to ourselves at the same time that with the help of his old friends, Mr. Mosely and Squire Pemberton, we would before the summer passed by, spend an hour's labor on the last resting place of Thomas Affleck.

9.

The Calvinistic Baptists were organized early, probably not long after the Presbyterians. We don't propose, however, to give a history of their church, nor of any of their preachers except Mr. Newport, and of him it is with regret we state that our material is so limited and imperfect. The generation of to-day know of him only by tradition, but that tradition, shaped as it may be, proves that its subject was a person of high public interest. The Rev. Richard Newport first began preaching for the Baptists of this country about 1839 or '40. His energy and great ability soon made him the pride and idol of his brethren. He could hold the largest congregations for three hours at a stretch and then stop from exhaustion only. He read the Bible much, having little or no school education, entertained the opinion that all other book knowledge was useless; that the concentration of mind and thought upon sacred subjects, matured and strengthened the light and power of spiritual discernment in God's elect. This opinion on the subject of spiritual illumination, so common then, and for what we know popular yet, had convinced Mr. Newport that he had received a divine call to preach the gospel;

and believing that a divine call meant pure and unadulterated Calvinism, he held, therefore, that the Armenian's claim to the same office by the same process was a fraud and a swindle.[1]

The right of private judgement on things divine has been popular for centuries, but even among the Baptists and other kindred faiths it has had its disadvantages. The neophyte may happen to have a good opinion of himself or rather of his powers of discernment, and as he reads along he is liable to make discoveries. Discoveries new and important to himself and worth telling to the church, as he supposes. After hearing Mr. Newport on one occasion, we witnessed a member rise and read to the congregation, an "Article of Faith" of his own composition, which was respectfully referred for future action. In a farmer's house we once picked up and looked into an eighty page pamphlet, setting forth Elder Daniel Parker's views or proofs of his "two seed" doctrine.[2] As we laid it back on the table, the owner remarked, "I believe every word in that discourse to be true." This monstrosity prevailed among the Baptists for "a year and a month and for a week and a day."

Mr. Newport's powers of invective together with his intemperate habits naturally caused criticism, probably the best advertisement he could have had. His answer was a denial in general, coupled with the consolation that the world ever had since the Apostles' day, and ever would hate light and the truth, and therefore would persecute and lie about its ministers. He rejoiced that he was held worthy of the world's hatred, for his reward would be the greater. On this subject we once heard him say "I say," and he repeated it, "I say any man must be a start-natur'l fool who will go out into the world calkerlatin' to preach

1. Dr. Rutherford was referring to *Arminianism*. This teaching, which developed from the writings of Jacobus Arminius (1560–1609), was an attack upon Calvinism. Arminianism greatly influenced Charles and John Wesley.

2. Daniel Parker (?–1844), a Baptist minister, moved to southern Illinois in 1817. He set forth his "Two-Seeds-in-the-Spirit" predestinarian doctrine in 1826. According to Parker, God "had created Adam and Eve with good seed emanating from divine origins. After man's fall from grace, however, 'seeds of the serpent' were also planted in Eve. Subsequent generations of mankind stem from one of these two sources, good and evil or elect and non-elect." Henry Warner Bowden, *Dictionary of American Religious Biography*, p. 351.

the gospel in its purity, and expect at the same time to be popular." Mr. Newport showed considerable skill in his treatment of his audiences. He usually commenced his sermons in a rambling sort of "point no point" talk without a Bible. His great memory served every purpose, as he quoted a passage here and there he gradually warmed up, getting deeper and deeper as he went. Finally he would blunder accidentally as it were upon a passage or word, and forthwith take it for a text. The longest sermon we ever heard him preach was upon the word "Salvation." Of course we cannot attempt to reproduce anything about it except a few of our faded impressions. This subject he held to be one of superior importance, and the momentous question would occur, he said, to the hearer, what is it and how is it attained? On the latter point he assumed and proved that his views ("hard shell,"[3] as people call them,) were correct, and as a matter of course all others were erroneous. Warming up with his work, he thoroughly condemned the timid and weak-kneed, halters between two opinions, among whom he enumerated the Presbyterians and what he designated as bastard Baptist sects. He called them lame ducks—maimed and blind—and finally consigned them to "shame and everlasting contempt." He next took hold of the Armenian for whom he entertained neither respect nor consideration, and in a very brief space of time ground him to absolute powder. Having cleared this rubbish out of his way as he called it, there then opened up to him as it were, bright lights and a clear sky, a new heaven and a new earth, which he pictured with a rapidity of utterance and earnest vehemence, that sent the froth and saliva from him over a portion of the audience. Swaying his great massive frame to and fro, he broke into a song of praise and triumph, passing thence into a recitative rhapsody, the tones of his voice rising and falling as he proceeded in regular cadence with the notes and bars of his refrain. Thus he held his audience spellbound till exhaustion compelled him to stop.

It is claimed as a matter of history, that preaching in this style—the "Sing Song" or "Tone," as the vulgar call it—took its

3. The "hard shell," or primitive Baptists, were strong Calvinists.

origin with a Presbyterian clergyman in the valley of Virginia, about 1740 or '50. Holding, however, to the opinion that as there is nothing new under the sun, this curious mode of preaching—which was successfully used also by the late Rev. John Shields—has in our opinion, its prototype in the liturgy of the Episcopal and Catholic churches. He who visits a Jewish synagogue will recognize in the ancient service of that people, much that is similar. The Psalms of David are an example, and the song of Miriam no doubt had its power in the same musical measure.

Mr. Newport lived in what is called the "rich woods" of Clark County. There he followed farming for a living, for he held in accordance with the faith of his brethren, that it was wrong to receive pay for preaching; hence his ministrations were literally "without money and without price." In his clerical services we had noticed in him as it were, two different acquirements. Whilst his discourses or sermons were, as the reader may have inferred, delivered in his vernacular—the south-western lingo of that day—his prayers on the contrary were moulded in the purest of scripture language. We have heard him often; once in particular at the residence of the elder Mrs. Sargent, where in a prayer of nearly twenty minutes in length, he committed not one error, either in grammar or expression.

It is said that one of the rules of the Baptist society, forbids its members from joining any other society not in affiliation with it. Unanimously, as it seems, these very excellent people disapprove of temperance societies, whilst at the same time their individual views or reasons on the subject, are various and sometimes very curious. We will mention two. The late Rev. John Shields held, as he once stated to us, that he regarded the existence of Sunday school and temperance organizations, as an evidence of the "last days," and as a forerunner of the Apocalyptic beast. Mr. Newport and very many others held that the evils and temptations of life were decreed and necessary tests of virtue— probationary training—and should be met in open field, with a square front, instead of avoiding or sneaking by them. It was in accordance with this lofty sentiment that the vestals of "virgins" of the primitive church acted. In the elegant language of Gibbon "they permitted priests and deacons to share their beds, to prove to themselves and the world that their virtue was invulnerable." "Be strong," was the rallying cry of Tecumseh in his last battle. "Resist the adversary and he will flee from you." This is the premise; what is the corollary? "Alas for poor human nature." Mr. Newport was not equal to the occasion in his encounter with corn juice; like the ancient "virgins," he came out of the hand to hand contest second best. His ability to perform the acrobatic feat, of taking just enough and no more, was conceded to be an impossibility.

Not long after his removal to Missouri, the rumor came back that he had there joined a temperance society. This astonishing news proved true, and we have learned from a reliable source, that he gave the following curious reason for it: Having once made an appointment to preach at a certain point, he thought it best before starting, to take into him a good dose of "fortification" by way of a stiffener. As he proceeded on his way he discovered that he had taken too much, and rode on very slowly hoping the effects would pass off in time for his appointment. Getting worse instead of better, and deeming himself unfit to appear before the people, he sought the friendly shelter of a deserted cabin by the road side. Hitching his horse he entered this lonely abode. It had no shutter to the door, no chinkin in the walls,[4] no floor nor roof. Underneath him were the old sleepers, above him were the bare ridge poles. The sun was high and he thought he would wait. Stretching himself between two sleepers with his head to the shady side of the wall, he fell asleep, and dreamed of snakes, and toads, and bats and other harmless creatures. Finally he dreamed that the Devil had come for him, and that he could distinctly hear the sound of his wings. Filled with terror and alarm he awoke; the sun was just then setting, its last rays were coming in through the open logs of the house, and the shades of evening were fast closing in. A slight noise caused him to look up, and there perched upon the ridge pole sat a turkey buzzard peering and looking down upon him

---

4. Cracks between the logs were chinked with small boards and then plastered over with mud.

with evident curiosity. The association of his dream with that foul bird, and his own shame and degradation filled him with horror. The idea that he had been mistaken for carrion transported him, not aloft but to the valley of humiliation, and so gathering himself up he put back home. He signed the pledge the next day, and it is a matter of fact and rejoicing for his old friends to know that he adhered to it and at last filled a sober man's grave.

10.

Odds and Ends

The reader may have noticed that the material of these papers relates mainly to individuals, to persons of a striking or peculiar cast of character, whilst the direct history of the village has so far occupied but a subordinate position. The leading interest in trading communities is generally the mercantile, and as we possess no manufactories—for the distillery of Davis & Co. was never revived—we devote a portion of this paper, to the rise and progress of the mercantile class in Oakland. We have seen in our veracious history, that the two stores of McClelland & Trembly closed up in 1840. The hardness of the times and the scarcity of money compelled a suspension. Deeply in debt to Cincinnati houses, these men could not pay and could not get credit. They therefore set to work collecting from their customers, anything and everything they could sell or turn into money. Hogs for the Terre Haute market, cows for the Chicago. In this sort of force-put position, they had to give or allow liberal prices on their accounts; prices so high, that when they got their stock to market, a heavy margin appeared against them. It is true that they sold their goods at a very great advance, yet the loss in collecting was so decided, that when McClelland died, he left a bankrupt estate; and Mr. Trembly though more fortunate, left the country worse off than when he came to it. For the next four years no goods of any kind, save what a peddler might bring in, were sold in Oakland. Our trading had to be done in Charleston or Paris. We remember once of carrying a broom on horseback from the latter place home. Not a spool nor a thread or even a pin was to be had short of these towns. One morning Mr. Chadd, from the country, came on search of two ounces of turpentine, and although he proclaimed that he had the money to pay for it, it was not to be obtained. There was nothing here to buy goods with. Four year old steers went at ten dollars per head, and the only good horse we ever owned we bought for fifty dollars. Corn for many years never rated above ten cents per bushel, and then was not considered a merchantable article. In the first year of our business, we booked over a thousand dollars and collected fifteen in cash. But those dreary days at last began to lighten, and as the wheel of time would keep turning it brought up Mr. Robert Moseley to the front. This gentleman opened out a small stock in May, 1844, and had the little trade, such as it was, to himself for a couple of years. John Mills and R. T. Hackett next tried their hands in a small trading stock, taking in butter, etc., wagoning it to Lafayette, for market. In the meantime, Matt Ashmore, who had bought Mr. Pemberton's old tavern, opened out a sort of "curiosity shop," which he kept in a style and order that would have given our friend Mr. Kurtz, a stroke of apoplexy to have seen it. After raising corn one season, Squire Pemberton went into partnership with Mr. Moseley, and the year 1847 was signalized by the beginning of their long partnership business. Competition, as we intimated, was pretty lively and the amount of wit bestowed by one firm upon the others, was mutual and pretty evenly balanced. In the matter of romance and storytelling, our old friend Robert had a decided advantage. Mills would turn up his nose when he heard his tales, and Matt would exclaim, "Well-now-Bob, why,-that's-vulgar!" We are sorry to say that a great many of these stories were in the style of Barney Russel, and as Lyman Keyes often said, "hadn't ought-to-been told."

Trade and farm prices becoming better, we soon lost a large part of our hunter population. These people led in most part a do-less, roving life, while the game lasted. When they came to town they carried a gun, carried one when they went visiting, and if they stepped over to a neighbor's on Sunday, the gun was sure to be taken along; "because," as Mike House observed, "a body might see a snake or some other varmint." Rough men have rough ways. Police and city marshals were not invented in this village, and on public days three or four fights was the common average. We have seen rings formed fifty feet wide, and have seen the belligerents stripped and spoiling for a fight, cavort and cave round the privileged enclosure, in a most alarming manner. Fortunately the spirit affected but one of them at a time, the other being quiet and waiting for something to "turn up," perhaps. No. 1 having blown off, No. 2 took up the refrain and went through the same performances whilst No. 1 "rested." We once saw an eager patient crowd break its ring in disgust at a game of this character, whilst Mr. Daugherty boiling over with contempt, proclaimed them "dung hills." As the sequel of a shooting match on another interesting occasion, a ring was formed by a select few who remained after the target practice of the day, to enjoy some whiskey and sugar at night. The snow covered the ground several inches deep "as with a mantle." The full moon shone down in steady brightness, whilst the quiet people of the village having retired, were snoring the night away in blessed unconsciousness—sleeping the sleep of the just. At this momentous juncture Jonathan Wayne and Lyman Keyes, passed within the precincts of the ring, rolling up their sleeves and looking hostile exceedingly at each other. "For what reason did you strike my boy?" enquired Wayne. "Well, the d——d whelp," replied Keyes, "drank my whiskey and stole my sugar." "You're a liar!" And a blow was the rejoinder, and both of them being light-bodied men, they tusselled around with considerable vigor. All this time the ring composed of Daugherty, Dick Hawkins, Lindly Ashmore, and a few others, with guns on their shoulders, kept dancing about calling "fair play, fair play." It had happened that the ring embraced in its bounds a few scattering sticks of Squire Pemberton's wood pile, and as the combatants kept pushing about, Keyes tripped over one of these snow covered sticks and came to the ground. As he fell his neck and back of his head rested upon another good sized stick. In this comfortable position, Wayne, with one hand on this throat, crowded down upon him and struck at his face repeatedly. The members of the ring looked on intently and waited for Lyman to cry

"Cavey," but his body was shadowed so much by his antagonist, that they finally came to the conclusion that the pressure on his throat prevented him, and so they separated them at once. When they stood up in the moonlight Lyman's face was untouched and unhurt, but Wayne's hand, which had by mistake come against the wood, had to be nursed for a week.

The old still house had its memories in the administration of justice. Every week when a "run" was on hand, more or less fighting would grace the occasion or else an accident would happen instead. Dan ———— had been testing the quality of the "run," but like Mr. Archer, he took too much of it and it flew to his head. Sauntering around amongst the mash tubs he was observed to be emptying his stomach, into one of these vessels. To assist him, Old Yaller kindly took a stern hold on him, jerked him suddenly up but unfortunately balancing over, he went down into the mash head foremost with his feet projecting above. Yaller called for help and got Dan partly out but he slipped back. On the next effort many hands being by this time laid upon him, he came out with a rush bringing a great flood of mash with him. Dan was removed to an old stable to repair damage, carrying with him the sympathies of the spectators, and the excuses and regrets of Old Yaller. As Dan sat in that old stable drying himself, with his head down, and his hair and clothing filled with the wet meal, we certainly never did see a more comical-looking individual. A couple of ladies called to see him, but Dan wouldn't look up and that night he made tracks and has never been heard of since.

Returning to our mercantile friends, we believe the late G. W. Ashmore, comes next in order of time. Mr. A. removed the Davis & Swall whiskey house, and put up a two story building with a store room below and hall above. This was if we remember rightly, in '52. Mr. A. sold goods in this house for a number of years and then traded his stock to Mr. Clement. Finally after much changing the house burnt down, and the bank building was erected on its site. Before this house was finished Mr. Ashmore died. Our friend D. W. Mitchell, who never will have a gray hair on his head, built his house on the opposite corner, much on the pattern of Mr. Ashmore, and went into the dry goods business in 1853. Excepting a few short intervals, Mr. Mitchell has continued steadily in that line ever since, selling "the cheapest goods that ever was sold." About the same time Dr. Wampler bought out the old tavern, and put up the shell of the present hotel, and built a store house on the opposite corner in which he sold goods. Selling out to Sam Ashmore, the latter kept store for some time, much after the fashion of the old lady who kept tavern. And now the dishonored building stands on the alley, devoted to miscellaneous uses, whilst its old site is occupied by T. S. Coffin's new brick with iron front.

In 1855, the brothers, L. S. and S. M. Cash bought out Moseley & Pemberton, and for two years sold goods in their old stand, where Williams & Carter now measure tape. From thence they moved to their new business house on the south side of the square where the law and whiskey den formerly stood. This building was burnt down a few years ago, and has been succeeded by their magnificent brick with stone front. In the long period of twenty-two years, this prosperous firm has never suspended nor closed up; an evidence of prosperity and steadiness in business which speaks for itself. Our community has lately had the misfortune to lose the younger member of this co-partnership of whom it may appropriately be said in the verse of Halleck

> Green be the turf above thee,
> Friend of my better days;
> None knew thee but to love thee,
> Nor named thee but to praise.

11.

John Richman, A Typical Backwoodsman

Looking backward is the office and duty of history. Its labors are to mark the milestones of time as they pass, and to grave upon them the record of days, of years and of ages, in their successive chronology. Looking backward, recalling a youthful epoch, the reminiscences of a past generation, is the pleasing task of old age, and it is in that line I would ask attention to a few incidents connected with the life and character of a noted man in the early history of Douglas County.

It was back in February, 1841, that a settler on Brush Creek, three miles southeast of Oakland, had a sale. He had had hard luck as he termed it. He had followed the rainbow to Illinois, but now the bow of promise was in Missouri, resting over the new Platte Purchase. There was snow on the ground, and taking a seat in a friend's sleigh, we made our way through the jack-oak brush to the place of sale.

Being a new comer myself, my object was to make acquaintance. But few people were present and a few more from various points kept dropping in; notably two from the head of the timber, one of whom was Captain James Bagley.

The sale of old barrels and other trumpery went slowly on. People cared more to group and gossip. A man in one of the groups near me, looking up the road, enquired, "Who's that?" No one knew the strange-looking person approaching. Captain Bagley being appealed to, said: "That's old John Richman." Mr. Richman was a man of sixty years, six feet high, strongly built and in vigorous health. He carried a long rifle—a deer gun—with a leather guard over the lock. His rig and costume were unique and picturesque even for that day; a full hunter's outfit. He wore no hat, but instead a knitted woolen cap of white, red and green bands, with a white tassel at the top. His hunting shirt was of walnut jeans fringed along the seams and skirts, and around the neck and cape. His pants, of the same material, were held up by a draw string and secured at the ankles by deer leather leggins, bound by cross thongs fastened to his moccasins. He wore a leather belt in which was stuck a small tomahawk. To his shoulder strap was attached a pouch, a powder horn and a small butcher knife in a sheath. His moccasins had sole leather bottoms fastened by thongs. He was clean shaved, and his shirt and clothing were bright and clean; a cleanly man by the way, and I never saw him in any other condition.

After greeting, he stated that one of his pet deer had escaped from his park three weeks ago. He had expected it to return, but, instead, found it had gone down the timber. He was sure it would come back in four weeks time, but fearing somebody might shoot the "critter," he had started out to find it and bring it back if alive. He had staid last night with his friend, Andrew Gwinn, and hearing of this sale, he had come by, hoping to hear of it. It was a doe with a red flannel band on its neck and with a small brass bell held by a leather strap. He added "If I could only hear one tinkle of that bell, I'd know it." No one had seen or heard of it, but all assured him that nobody would kill it, knowing from the band that it was a pet. Some one suggested that as the truant was going down the river, she might still be on the tramp, and by this time be in Jasper County. He shook his head with a decisive "No! She will not go more than two miles below here." He gave no reason for the opinion, but he no doubt knew what we did not know, that the range limit for the deer was twenty miles from the place of birth and breeding. I would remark here, in parenthesis that all animals—man excepted— have their range limits. Naturalists tell us that the deer and antelope species have twenty miles, the lion and tiger ten, the horse five, the wolf four, the cow three, the hog two, the dog one, the cat a half, and the rabbit, like the hen and the quail, spend their lives on forty acres. Some one else inquired, "How will you find that deer amongst the brush, the thickets and the long grass?" Holding up a turkey call-bone he said, "Every day when I brought her her feed, I called her up with that bone; if ever she hears it again she will know it and come to me. She will know me, too, and let me lead her home. If she is alive I will find her and find her down there"—pointing to the southwest. I had read with the ardor of youth, "Gertrude of Wyoming" and the "Leather Stocking Tales." I had heard of Mr. Richman before and now realized that there stood before me a type of a mountain hunter, more perfect, perhaps, than any that fiction had ever made. Shouldering his gun, he went on his way. We watched him with interest till he disappeared among the trees in his loving search for the lost doe.

It subsequently transpired that he made his way to the neighborhood of St. Omar, two miles north of Ashmore. Here, he decided, was the deer's boundary limits, here he began his search, as I was told afterwards by several of the residents. He staid two days roaming over the barrens and river bluffs, sounding his call-bone as he went, but no doe ever came to him. He became convinced that some one had killed it, and the wretch who had done it lived near by. In his anger he told several people what he thought and that if he ever found out who did it, he would put a bullet through him if it was seven years afterwards. He made and repeated this savage declaration in the house of David Golliday, Sr., unaware of the fact that at that time the band and bell of his doe was then hidden within a few feet of him. A few days previous one of the Golliday boys had brought in the dead body of the truant doe, with the red band and bell on it; knowing how mean and dirty the act was, the family kept it secret. The old man's threats terrified them so much that the bell was kept in hiding for several years, till it was known that the ferocious old hunter was dead.

In the summer of 1842 I happened to pass by the house of Mr. Richman. His son David and his young wife were living there. The old man, being a widower, lived with them. I was called in to minister to a sick child. The house was a rudely constructed affair. It had a puncheon floor, an outside stick chimney, and the house corners were untrimmed. It stood by the calamus patch in the fair grounds. Mr. Richman, the elder, at that time, was particularly busy. As was his habit, he sat upon the floor with a deer skin under him, tanned with the hair on, and the neck, tail and legs clipped off. In his hand he held a piece of chair rung, to the end of which was attached a piece of sole leather, forming a convenient paddle. With this deadly weapon he slaughtered every fly he could reach adding at each successful blow a suitable curse adjective. A pair of short boards, leaning together at top and smeared with honey, stood on a shelf as a fly trap. Every few minutes he would rise from the floor and bring the trap together with a bang, supplemented with a furious "There, damn ye!" by way of comment. This is the opposite of romance, Fenimore Cooper never degraded his hunters and warriors to such small game; but all the same, such is life, such is reality. It was said of Mr. Richman that he would sit for hours at a time by his bee hives killing drones. The Oriental practice of sitting on the floor, as a comfortable and easy posture, has ever been a puzzle to us of the West. In the course of his fly campaign he sat down and rose up many times; and what is singular, he did it with ease and grace, such as long practice alone can give. I had seen him once before sit for hours on that deer skin, and what is more, had seen him sleep on it, too, his head and shoulders lightly leaning against a table.

One day in November, '44, Mr. Richman appeared at my house, telling me he had a job for me. Stripping up his sleeve, he exhibited a wen on his upper arm, as large as a turkey egg. He said he had tried two faith doctors on it, but did no good, adding, "The sign wasn't right, or sumthin'. Could I cut it out for him?" To my inquiry as to when he wished it removed, he said in his decided way, "It must be done to-day or to-morrow, because the sign to-day is in the legs and to-morrow it'll be in the feet. After that it'll be in the head again, and you know it wouldn't do then at all; it 'ud be dangerous." The wen therefore was removed at once. As the wound bled slightly he became uneasy, remarking that he had the power to "stop blood" on other people but could not on himself. He could "learn a woman," however, to do it, and if I would permit my wife to go into the back yard with him, he would learn her to stop the flow. Nodding assent, they retired—it would ruin the charm for me to see or hear the process—and he had her place her fingers over the wound, repeating after him a pow-wow formula commanding the flow to stop in the name of God and his holy angels. As there was no apparent result and he seemed anxious, I did what I should have done at first, put on another and tighter bandage. But Mr. Richman was satisfied, nevertheless, that the "words" had done the business.

He staid with me two days and told me a hundred of his hunting, mining and ghost stories. Brim full of superstitions, he was what the scriptures call a "natural man." Without moral or religious training, he did not know one letter from another, and to him the reading of a printed page was a mystery. His youth and manhood had been spent in the mountains of Virginia, living a wild and savage life. He told me he had never worn a shoe or a boot nor ever had an overcoat on his back. Roaming over the country in search of game, in those days when the prairie was a wilderness and the settler was found only at distant points of timber, it was his habit when night was coming down, to make his way to the nearest cabin in sight, *sans ceremoni*, without a knock, he lifted the latch, walked in and made himself at home. To the lonely settler he was always a welcome guest, a God-send in fact. In his dialectic vernacular he repeated to his eager listeners his old time adventures—a light sleeper, he literally "sat by the fire and talked the night away."

From the late Andrew Gwinn I learned that his father was a woodsman by profession, what the French term a *courier de bois*.[1] As a scout he served under Lord Dunmore and fought the Indians under Cornstalk at the battle of Point Pleasant. John was his eldest son and had the good fortune to marry a woman of exceptional wisdom and patience. It was said of her that no other woman could control his passionate fits. They were energetic, industrious and prosperous. Deciding to live in the Wabash country, they spent a year in preparation. Two great poplar trees, made two large canoes. These dugouts were launched on New River, placed catamaran fashion, a deck was built over them, and pitching his tent on top, with his family inside, the craft floated down the river. Down the Kanawha, down the Ohio to the mouth of the Wabash. In the low water of summer he and his sons pushed that flotilla up stream, day after day, till they reached Eugene. They staid here a couple of years, as I have understood, living in the tent, and in the spring of 1829, moved to the Ambraw. Mr. Richman has ever since carried the distinction of being the first settler in Douglas County. The exact date is to me unknown.

It may be stated here as an item of county history, that Captain Samuel Ashmore in that same year located in Sargent township on what is known as the Sargent farm. His son, Omer, living in Iowa, writes me that they came to a halt on the 15th day of May. His father had two wagons, five yoke of cattle and a pair of horses. They immediately broke up twenty acres, planted and fenced it, housing themselves in the covered wagon. The next thing in order was a house. The late Geo. Ashmore told me that

1. Dr. Rutherford's spelling for *coureur des bois*.

his father sent him up to Richman's for help, and the next day Mr. Richman and four of his sons came down to assist in the raising. In that year but these two families were in the county, and it is quite certain that this was the first house in the county. House building items of an early date have an interest for every locality. The late Young E. Winkler stated that his mother and his brother Edmund came to Brushy Fork in 1830. They built the first house at what is known as the north end of the Hopkins bridge. The little clearing is there yet, and the house to my recollection stood there tenantless for many years. Ed moved from there to the Albin farm. In the fall of that year Mr. Winkler came to Brushy on a visit; from there he rode over to Richman's. They were still living in the big tent. Old John, as he was called, had at that time six bee trees marked in the woods. Mr. Winkler tried to buy one, but could not. Mr. Richman had scruples, thought it would be an act of betrayal, which the bees might avange by a spell on him, rendering it impossible to ever find another hive.

The Richman boys were quite peaceable men, much like their mother in disposition. John and David had her dark hair and personally resembled her. All had more or less of their father's disposition. When David lay in his last illness, he told me he wished to sell out; hoped to get six dollars per acre for his little farm, hoped to get well, to go to Oregon, to the Rocky Mountains to hunt the bear, the elk and the blacktailed deer. Of his five sons, I thought Lewis, the youngest, resembled his father the most.

Discussing this point once with the late James Hammet, he disagreed with me, but to me, the resemblance, if not striking, was considerable. Alike in size and build, both had sandy hair, the same piping voice and the same wild staring look.

As a sequel to my sketch of this wild man of the woods, permit me to close with an anecdote told me long ago by the Rev. John Steel, of Grandview, Edgar County. Mr. Steel was born on the Greenbrier River in Virginia, near the Richmans and knew the family well, especially the younger members of it. He stated that a new church had been built in the neighborhood, seated in pew style, finished and dedicated. On a summer's Sabbath day services had been opened, the preacher had started into his sermon, when a strange man in hunter's garb was seen standing in the doorway, eyeing the preacher with intense earnestness. He was recognized as Bill Richman, a brother to John. After a long pause, he stretched forth his long arm and grasped the pew railing, drawing one foot forward followed by the other. Then another reach with one foot at a time, never moving his eye from the preacher for a moment. Arriving at a vacant pew, he raised one moccasined foot, passed it over the door to the inside floor, then the other and sat down. He remained seated about ten minutes, then rose, passing one foot over the door outside, then the other as he stood in the aisle, all the time keeping his alert eyes upon the preacher as danger point. He then moved backward by reaches, along the railing as he had advanced, till he stood on the doorsill. Then with one last wild, staring look at the preacher, he sprang backward and out several feet, turned hastily and disappeared in the adjoining forest.

12.

Jonas Bragg—A Personal Sketch

According to the Norse-Tutonic mythology, Jotun (Hell) is situated in the far north; a land of rock, snow, ice and perpetual fog. The sun never shines there, the souls of the bad and especially the coward, or those who have shrunk the ordeal of the battle field have their eternal home in that uncomfortable place.

Asgard (Heaven) is a land of flowers, trees, grassy meads and flowing streams. In this sunshiny Paradise the brave, the good and the true have their residence and drink mead as the ages roll by. But in Asgard is a celestial mansion, a holy of holies, a new Jerusalem, reserved for heros who have fallen on battle fields. It is called Val Halla (Hall of the chosen). It has 365 doors and as many windows. It is approached by the Rain-bow bridge. Hierndall keeps the doors; he is the son of Nine Sisters; his senses are so acute that he can hear the grass grow, and see all things.

The battle maids bring the warriers over the bridge and into the Hall where the boar Schrimer is slain. They wait upon the warriers, bring them tit bits of the flesh with flagons of holy mead for refreshments. The great Gods Odin, Thor and Fry preside over the feast. Lesser gods and goddesses are present to honor the assembly. Notably among these is Braggi; he is the god of Romance, poetry and song. In his hands he holds the sacred Zeither and as he sounds its strings, he chants and sings the praises of the great gods and of the lesser, but especially of the warriers before him. He tells of all their great and mighty deeds, how they handled the sword, the bow and the spear. He tells to their credit of much and many things that never happened. A very popular individual is Braggi. Beside him sits his wife, the beautiful Nanno. She is the goddess of perpetual youth, and at her feet is a basket filled with the golden apples of immortality.

Away back in the far away Norseland and in the far away times the great Bragg family were warriers bold and took spoil with the strong hand. In the pursuit of happiness and plunder they sailed down the great North sea, till they came to the sea of glass, where they stopped to pay respect to Grimhilda, the daughter of Odin in the city of Iss. The romance of that distinguished lady is told in "Der Nederlungenlied" but space forbids further notice of her. The sea of glass is there still, bright and clear and so too is her city of Iss upon its shores. Geographers now call it Callais—place of the lily—to distinguish it from its great sister—Paris—the place of the Spear.[1]

Passing over to Britain they scattered in that unknown land and as the centuries rolled by they drifted into those occupations common to Medieval times. Musicians, Henchmen, Harpers, pilgrims and rovers. Some of them crossed the Atlantic and one found his way over the mountains to the Greenbrier valley. This Bragg was a philosopher, whose thoughts were of today; to him tomorrow was an unknown quantity. A happy-go-lucky man after Pope's model, whose wishes and cares were bounded by a very few acres and a very few other things. His legacy to the world was a widow and ten sons.

1. We were unable to determine what Norse-Teutonic mythology Dr. Rutherford read. We have retained his inventive spellings.

Jonas Bragg was one of this decimal family, and as I first saw him in 1841 was a man of perhaps forty years of age, whose unique appearance was striking. Black hair and beard was relieved by a long aquiline nose surmounted by the worst squint eye that ever was seen. A great wide mouth, no chin, narrow chest, slightly stooping and five foot ten. He introduced himself by saying, "I am Bragg by name and brag by nature, I am a stockman and believe in good blood. I feel sure the Braggs have good blood in them; good Virginia blood. My father was a poor man and could not give us education, but poverty don't kill blood! No sir, we have it. When we came to this country, we wagoned down the Kanawa to Point Pleasant. The Ohio was booming and we had to wait two days before crossing. To kill time I sauntered round the town and then down to the old fort. There I saw Mrs. General Armstrong and her two daughters picking wool. They were poor, but the noblest looking women I ever saw; they had the best of Virginia blood in them. No sir, poverty don't kill blood!" Having a "call" farther up the timber we rode up the river road on the west side. Coming to a little enclosed space with a double log cabin in it, and some children about the door, Mr. Bragg drew up his horse by the fence, and remarked: "This is where I live; I am a widower and those two girls are my house keepers, and they do first rate; they are twelve and fourteen years old." I have a pleasant recollection of those girls and kept trace of them till they married and passed out of sight. "That boy standing against the tree is my eldest child, Aleck. He is sixteen and has made one horse swap; made a good one too, and I did not help him either; No sir." To the remark, "that boy will make his way in the world," he replied, "Yes, I think so, I hope he will have better luck than his father."

Mr. Bragg was not what the world calls a successful man. "A rolling stone gathers no moss." During the twenty years that I knew him I never found him twice in the same house. It was reported of him that he had moved his residence four times in one year. But the man's genuine goodness of heart, and the comicality of his ways, foibles and acts, made him a "character." Men of character are those we remember most about, think about and write about.

In the Greenbrier country there were no free schools and Mr. Bragg could neither read nor write. A false pride caused him to ignore the fact which every body knew. I have repeatedly heard him speak of writing and reading letters and newspapers. His skill in avoiding a signature was wonderful. I once witnessed a remarkable instance of this kind, [but] I will give one told me by the late Washington Williams. "When in the summer of 1842, Mr. Bragg came over to Vermillion to marry one of my elder sisters. My brother John told him he would have to obtain a license at Danville. It was arranged for brother John to go, but an order being necessary he said, 'Just write it out for me,' which was done and handed to him for signature. 'All right,' said Bragg, looking the paper over carefully, 'all right, just put my name to it, you have the pen, all right!'" Mr. Williams made this remark about it, "Boy as I was at the time, I noticed that he held the writing upside down!"

Mr. Bragg was a very impulsive individual. Aside from change in residence he varied his occupations and was swift on new schemes. When a religious revival was got up, Bragg was sure to join, and was a liberal contributor, but by the time the six months probation was ended, something else had captured his mind, so that he failed of regular church membership. Somehow, inadvertently, of course, he'd get outside the traces and be "drop'd." In the early 50's he had made an effort in this direction, and Mr. Bragg most earnestly endeavored to hold out the probationary term. But unfortunately the Central Railroad had been opened to Champaign, and Mr. Bragg had engaged in the Chicago horse trade. Mr. B. was a great lover of horses and at that time resided on what was known as the Hut farm south of Camargo, where a big spring rose to the surface in the horse lot. The Methodist church of Camargo had at that time an iron clad discipline, and what is more, it was enforced. I believe it was Mr. Cole Bright who said they could give the old Puritans odds, then win; like their historic predecessors, their religious fervor, good works, and good intentions, did not save them from mistakes and blunders. A notice was left at Mr. Bragg's house requesting him to appear before the church class on the next Sabbath to answer a charge of blasphemy. Mr. B.

did not know what the word blasphemy meant, it was new to him; and with his usual caution in educational matters, consulted a friend. "What do they mean by that?" "They mean that you have been swearing, that's what they mean." "Bless you, no, that can't be it; I never swear. Nobody ever heard me swear. You never did? No, that's not it" and curious to know what was up, he met the class on time.

Rev. John Reynolds or Runnels as every body called him was the class leader, and opened the case by stating that he lived the next farm south of brother Bragg, that he had been told that brother Bragg was collecting horses for the Chicago market and had then a fine lot ready to ship. [Rev. Reynolds continued:] "I like to see good horses myself and so one Sunday morning after breakfast I went over to brother Bragg's to look at them. There was a big rail fence around the lot and a good many horses in it. Brother Bragg was standing in the middle of the lot, bare headed, in his shirt sleeves, with his arms folded and looking somewhere at something. I called to him through the fence and said, 'brother Bragg, I heard you had a lot of good horses and I thought I'd take a look at them.' Brother Bragg would have me climb the fence and look them over together with him. I think myself to be a fair judge of horses; I thought brother Bragg's a first class lot and I told him so. So far he had said but little, but remarked, 'I'm going to take into Chicago the best lot of horses that ever went into that city.' I thought the expression rather steep, but said nothing. 'Brother Runnels,' said he, 'you haven't seen them all yet. Come with me and I'll show you the best horse you ever saw.' The horse was standing near the fence on the west side of the lot. I have seen a good many first class horses, but I confess I have never seen one equal to that one. He was a king among horses, and I told him so. Brother Bragg had said nothing, but he raised his hand and brought it down with a slap on the horses back, and as he did so, he said, 'that is an Almighty horse.' I immediately reproved brother Bragg and said, 'that is a very profane and wicked expression to compare or associate the Almighty with a horse. No christian nor no Methodist should ever do so. Its contrary to our church discipline.' Brother Bragg made no reply; he seemed to be thinking of other things. He raised his hand again and again brought it down on the horses back with a heavy slap, and as he did so he said, 'I tell you, brother Runnels, that is an Almighty horse.' I could have excused the first expression he made because I thought he did not know any better; but his using it again, after my reproof, was too much. My duty as class leader compelled me to lay it before the church. I live neighbor to brother Bragg, and during my life time, I have lived by a good many good neighbors; but I have never lived by a better one than brother Bragg. I have done my duty. I will not speak on this case nor vote on it, nor wait for your decision." And so it was this good and well meaning man took up his hat and left the house bowed with sorrow.

At this point, it may be remarked, parenthetically, as the reader no doubt has noticed, that the good old fathers and mothers of Camargo church generally, and brother Runnels in particular, were not grammarians. The technical distinctions, signification and relations of nouns and adjectives were to them unknown quantities. They had never read Lindly Murray.[2]

Mother Brewer was the first to speak upon the question. She had known brother Bragg long and favorably, and from the evidence of brother Runnels she felt sure there was no evil intended. On proper acknowledgement of fault on his part she thought the church could afford to forgive him and place him on his feet again. Others spoke to the same effect but desired to have brother Watson's views. Rev. W. D. Watson, the time honored local preacher, responded by saying in part, that blasphemy was a sin against God and against the church. The church had no power to forgive the sin against God but could do so only as related to itself. "The question is," [he concluded,] "shall we forgive brother Bragg; for my part, I coincide with sister Brewer. I know of no rule better than the one Christ laid down, when the Pharisee, referring to the Mosaic law, inquired of him, 'Shall I forgive my brother seven times?' His answer was,

2. Dr. Rutherford acquired his copy of Lindley Murray, *English Grammar, Adapted to the Different Classes of Learners* . . . (Baltimore: Armstrong & Plaskett, 1828), in 1833. The volume is now in the possession of his granddaughter, Mrs. Harriet Rutherford Crawford.

'Yea, not only seven times, but seventy times seven.'" Mr. Bragg was all ready to make the proper acknowledgement and apology, when Doctor Meadows rose to his feet. From what he had seen and heard, the Doctor said he was convinced that the Methodist church of Camargo was in a very bad way, going to the dogs as fast as it could: "We have before us an old trespasser, Jonas Bragg, always kicking over the traces, always violating the rules, and yet good and worthy members wish to take this mass of corruption back into good fellowship. When they do so, there is just one more thing to do as regards discipline: pull up stakes and quit the business." There had been a long smouldering feud between the two men, and Mr. Bragg flamed up at the Doctor's first word; his squint eyes looked unutterable things. "John Meadows," said he, "I know'd you in Virginia and I didn't know any good of you. You tattled and lied about me there and you've kept it up here, said mean things about me. You've said I had a white liver, and that I was a strange Jonas. Now this thing has gone on long enough; we'll settle it right now and here," shedding his coat and rolling up his sleeves before the astonished congregation. Mother Brewer promptly placed her burly form in front of her son-in-law[3] and with uplifted hands waved Mr. Bragg back. "Please, Mother Brewer, please step aside and let Meadows and I settle this matter." He tried to reach his game over her shoulders, but she waved him back. "Now don't, brother Bragg, don't now." Meadows sat there most provokingly cool, "Give him rope, mother, give him rope!" A flank movement on the old lady failed; she had the inner line, and realizing that he could do nothing, Mr. Bragg put down his sleeves, resumed his coat, muttering, "We'll have this out at another time and place," left the house in a towering rage, declaring he would belong to no church or society where Dr. Meadows was a member.

Notwithstanding his rolling stone habits, he did gather some moss, and rolled himself over to Urbana as a better business point. There like the man going to Jericho, he fell among thieves and returned to the Ambraw a poor man. I last saw him

3. Dr. Meadows.

in '61 keeping hotel in Camargo. He made no complaint, but the old time buoyant spirit was gone. Two years later he was laid to rest in the Hamet graveyard and his unique memory is all that remains of him. No better hearted man lies beneath the soil of Camargo township. Peace to his ashes! May we add the paraphrased prayer "Let his good deeds be graven in brass and his faults in water."

The Matson Slave Case

The Matson *Slave Case*

Dr. Hiram Rutherford was a major participant in the *Matson* slave case. Abraham Lincoln was his adversary, and had Lincoln won the case, the slaves would have been returned to servitude. This case has been called "one of the strangest episodes in Lincoln's career at the bar."[1] The basic facts are deceptively simple, but the human relationships and motivations are complicated and cannot now be completely understood.

Dr. Rutherford came from a Pennsylvania Abolitionist family. A "Conscience Whig," he was a strong believer in freeing the slaves. When he came to Illinois, he was probably not even aware of the state's so-called Black Law, which made it difficult for free blacks to reside in the state. One section of the law called for a fine of $500 for anyone harboring a "negro or mulatto" without a certificate of freedom.[2] This Black Law was seldom enforced, but it remained on the statute books until after the Civil War began.

Dr. Rutherford's entanglement with the Black Law came about in this way. In 1843, General Robert Matson of Bourbon County, Kentucky, bought a plot of land near Newman, Illinois, not far from Oakland, and called the farm Black Grove.[3] General Matson was a bachelor of about fifty, handsome, gentle-

1. Note in *Life on the Circuit with Lincoln*, p. 315.
2. See Jesse W. Weik, "Lincoln and the Matson Negroes, A Vista into the Fugitive Slave Days," p. 752.
3. Ironically, Matson's Black Grove farm is now owned by one of Dr. Rutherford's descendants.

manly, and a lover of the liquid refreshment of his Kentucky country. Like Dr. Rutherford, he was a Whig (but a Cotton Whig or Clay Whig, as the proslavers were called) and he became one of Dr. Rutherford's patients. General Matson was a slave owner in Kentucky, and each spring he would transport several of his slaves to his Illinois farm, returning them to Kentucky after the crops were harvested. Once the slaves arrived in Illinois, Matson would call in one of his white workers, Joe Dean, and swear that the slaves were in transit and would be sent soon to Kentucky. By this procedure Matson was attempting to preserve his legal ownership of slaves in a "free" state.

One Negro, the ancient Anthony Bryant, stayed on the Illinois farm the year around, acting as overseer, and he had apparently thus acquired his freedom. Anthony Bryant was married to a slave named Jane, who was reputedly the daughter of General Matson's brother. She had at least five children, and several of these children also had white fathers. In 1847 Jane Bryant and four of her children were among the slaves brought to work at Black Grove.

At the farm, Mary Corbin, a white woman, was housekeeper and also General Matson's mistress. She was a woman of temper, and during an argument with Jane Bryant, she threatened to influence Matson to have Jane and her children sold and sent "way down South in the cotton fields."[4] The threat greatly alarmed Jane and her husband. Anthony had a license as a Methodist "exhorter and local preacher," and his first thought was to seek help from his fellow Methodists. The Methodists in Charleston wished the frightened blacks well but were reluctant to interfere with General Matson's affairs. Anthony then went to the Methodist minister in Camargo for help, but the Reverend William Watson was a candidate for a seat in the legislature, and he did not want to damage his political chances by being called an Abolitionist. He wished them well and promised to pray for them, but he asked Anthony not even to mention the visit.[5]

4. Weik, p. 753.

5. P. T. McIntyre, "The Matson Slave Trial," Oakland *Weekly Ledger*, June 17, 1896. Collection of Austin Rutherford.

Anthony Bryant then rode into Oakland, and there he found two sympathetic citizens, Dr. Hiram Rutherford and Gideon Matthew ("Matt") Ashmore, a hotelkeeper and an ardent Abolitionist from a Tennessee family. In an interview with Jesse W. Weik, Dr. Rutherford gave this account of that meeting. "We told the frightened old negro to return to the Matson place and bring his family down to us, spiriting them away, if necessary, during the night. Realizing the danger of such a proceeding both to us and to the slaves, we quietly invoked the aid of a few discreet and fair-minded friends. The time had now come for us to show our hands. We met at the home of Ashmore, and had our forces within hailing distance by nine o'clock that night. We waited till midnight, when the party, father, mother, and one child, on horseback, the rest on foot, arrived, all excited and panting from their hurried journey across the prairie. They remained with us several days, although Matson and one of his trusted friends, Joseph Dean, endeavored by alternate appeals and threats to win them from our protection."[6] The next part of the story is best told by attorney D. T. McIntyre, who knew Dr. Rutherford well and had obviously heard Dr. Rutherford's narrative many times:

Ashmore and Rutherford, now the guardians of these otherwise friendless slaves, got into a buggy and drove to Charleston, where they laid the case before their mutual friend, Col. Ficklin [an attorney], and with good judgment took his advice. They returned to Oakland to await developments. All the while poor old Anthony and his enslaved wife were carefully cared for at Ashmore's hotel, without cost or charge therefor, little dreaming that they were to be the subjects of the romantic incidents which were soon to take place.

Upon every hand it was plainly visible that a storm of no small magnitude was brewing. Matson was making threats against both Rutherford and Ashmore. The great majority were in sympathy with these two heroes. The only question was, will they stand firm when the magnitude of the undertaking was fully realized. Matson was determined, and at that distant period the laws of the state seemed to be in his favor.

6. Weik, p. 754.

Everybody was waiting in suspense, but they did not have to wait long. In about two weeks the storm broke and the legal contest which was to determine the freedom of Jane and her children was to take place. It commenced by the issue of a writ by one William Gilman, a Justice of the Peace, commanding Jane and her children to appear before him forthwith and answer the claim of Robert Matson claiming their services as due to him, etc.

How absurdly preposterous such a proceeding seems to us, as we stand upon the summit of the civilization of the nineteenth century, and look back upon it! The idea that a poor ignorant Justice of the Peace should assume to sit in judgment upon the question of the freedom or bondage of five human beings would seem beyond the range of possibility. But strange as it would seem, it was nevertheless a veritable fact, and will forever stand as a burning blot upon not only the history of this county but that of the entire state of Illinois.

Immediately upon the service of this monumental writ Mr. Ashmore, wishing to conform to the laws, bundled Jane and her children into a wagon and himself drove them down to Charleston where they were, under pretext of being safely kept, lodged in jail and kept in confinement as felons until their new trial, which was set two days later.[7]

McIntyre explained that Justice of the Peace Gilman was proslavery and a friend of Usher Linder, Matson's attorney. Fearing certain defeat, Ficklin then called for two additional associates to hear the case with Gilman; of those two, Eastin was proslavery, while Shepherd sympathized with the position of Rutherford and Ashmore.

On the day of the trial, Ashmore and Rutherford announced that they were prepared, if necessary, to carry the case to the Supreme Court of the United States. The trial began with Joe Dean swearing that General Matson had sworn to him that the slaves were only temporarily at Black Grove and would be returned to Kentucky. McIntyre then comments: "On that evidence Linder tried to float the laws of Kentucky into the state of Illinois, calling it the law of the domicil following the master and

7. McIntyre.

his property wherever he went. . . . He threw all the force of his great forensic powers into his argument."[8]

Dr. Rutherford described the proceedings to McIntyre: "I have heard him [Linder] a hundred times but never knew him to make so great an effort. The court adjourned for dinner. Matson was elated; he and I boarded with Judge Cullom and ate at the same table. We were always on speaking terms and discussed our controversy in good humor. He had the manners of a gentleman. In the afternoon Mr. Ficklin made, by way of reply, as I think, the very best effort of his life."[9]

The activities outside the courtroom were reminiscent of scenes which were to occur in several Northern states immediately after the passage of the Fugitive Slave Law in 1851.[10] One such case involved an escaped slave named Shadrack who was arrested in Boston and was to be returned to his master in Virginia. An antislavery mob rescued him from jail and transported him to safety in Canada. Later that same year, a young escaped slave named Thomas Sims was arrested in Boston; Abolitionists attempted to rescue him, but the government used 250 troops to foil that attempt, and Sims was returned to Georgia. In Charleston, Illinois, these events were occurring, according to Dr. Rutherford's friend McIntyre:

Anticipating a verdict Joe [Dean, Matson's employee,] had procured a pair of horses, hitched them to the court house fence, had thoughtfully put straw in the bed of the wagon and was seen to put pieces of bed cord in, the design of which, as all knew, was to hustle Jane and the children inside, tie her and then he, with an assistant as driver, and James and Van Estin as horse-back guards, were to make a rush for the state line. While all this preparation was going on Dr. Rutherford and Ashmore were not idle either, and had organized a pursuing company of some eight or ten determined men. . . . They, like the Estins, had tied their horses to the court house

8. *Ibid.*
9. *Ibid.*
10. For an excellent account of the Fugitive Slave Law actions in Massachusetts, and Thoreau's reactions, see Walter Harding, *The Days of Henry Thoreau*, pp. 314–19.

fence awaiting the result, while pistols, guns, and other weapons were flouted dramatically in the air. Things now looked as if bloodshed were inevitable. The whole community was aroused to a fever heat, and it was plainly evident that in case the court should order Jane and her children to be returned into slavery desperate measures of resistance would surely be resorted to.

McIntyre concluded this section of the story by suggesting that Dr. Rutherford and Ashmore would have lost their case "had not the court become aware that the proceedings on the outside were not mere theories." The court ruled that it had no jurisdiction, and that Jane and the children should be returned to jail.[11]

After this exciting first trial, Joe Dean (called "infamous" and "white trash" by Dr. Rutherford's friends) was egged as he left town. General Matson was arrested—probably on charges brought by Dr. Rutherford and Ashmore or their supporters—and convicted for living with a mistress. Matson countered by suing Matt Ashmore and Dr. Rutherford for detaining his slaves and asked for their release by a writ of *habeas corpus*.

The following account of Dr. Rutherford, as transcribed by Weik, brings Lincoln into the dramatic action of the story:

Ashmore and I, having espoused the cause of the slaves, now fell under the shadow of Matson's wrath. His revenge culminated in a suit brought against us in the circuit court under the Black Law, demanding damages in the sum of twenty-five hundred dollars, or five hundred dollars for each slave. As soon as the summons was served on me I rode down to Charleston to hire a lawyer. I had known Abraham Lincoln several years, and his views and mine on the wrong of slavery being in perfect accord, I determined to employ him; besides, everyone whom I consulted advised me to do so. I found him at the tavern sitting on the veranda, his chair tilted back against one of the wooden pillars, entertaining the bystanders and loungers gathered about the place with one of his irresistible and highly-flavored stories. My head was full of the impending lawsuit, and I found it a great test of my patience to await the end of the chapter then in process of narration.

11. McIntyre.

Before he could begin on another I interrupted and called him aside. I told in detail the story of my troubles, reminded him that we had always agreed on the questions of the day, and asked him to represent me at the trial of my case in court. He listened attentively as I recited the facts leading up to the controversy with Matson, but I noticed a peculiarly troubled look came over his face now and then, his eyes appeared to be fixed in the distance beyond me, and he shook his head several times as if debating with himself some question of grave import. At length, and with apparent reluctance, he answered that he could not defend me, because he had already been counselled with in Matson's interest, and was therefore under professional obligations to represent the latter unless released. This was a grievous disappointment, and irritated me into expressions more or less bitter in tone. He seemed to feel this, and even though he endeavored in his plausible way to reconcile me to the proposition that, as a lawyer, he must represent and be faithful to those who counsel with and employ him, I appeared not to be convinced. I remember retorting that "my money was as good as any one's else," and although thoroughly in earnest I presume I was a little too hasty.[12]

Dr. Rutherford's account, long after the event, is notable for its sharp and clear details and for the generosity he showed in assuming some of the responsibility for the strained relations with Lincoln. Dr. Rutherford admitted that in his anger, he acted somewhat hastily in seeking another attorney. But why did Lincoln agree to appear for Matson? John J. Duff, in *A. Lincoln: Prairie Lawyer*, rightly observes that Lincoln's motivations will never be known.[13] Dr. Rutherford, undoubtedly from private conversations, thought that he and Lincoln agreed on the slavery issue, but did Lincoln fear being branded in public as a defender of Abolitionists? Whatever his reasons were, Lincoln was evidently troubled by his decision. Dr. Rutherford continued the story:

The interview and my quick temper, I am sure, made a

12. Weik, p. 755.

13. John J. Duff, *A. Lincoln: Prairie Lawyer*, p. 136. Duff's entire chapter on the Matson Slave Case is excellent.

deep impression on Mr. Lincoln, because, a few hours later, he despatched a messenger to me with the information that he had sent for the man who had approached him in Matson's behalf, and if they came to no more decisive terms than at first he would probably be able to represent me. In a very brief time this was followed by another message, that he could now easily and consistently free himself from Matson, and was, therefore, in a position, if I employed him, to conduct my defence. But it was too late; my pride was up, and I plainly indicated a disinclination to avail myself of his offer.[14]

Dr. Rutherford engaged Charles H. Constable, and Ashmore was represented by Orlando B. Ficklin. Lincoln and Usher Linder represented Matson. The case was heard in Circuit Court in Charleston by Judges Samuel Treat and William Wilson in October of 1847. According to Ficklin, the only one of the four lawyers to write about the case: "This was the hinge on which the case turned. Were the negroes held in transitue while passing over or crossing the state or were they located for a time by the consent of the master? If only crossing the state that act did not free them, but if located by the consent of the owner, even temporarily, that would emancipate them."[15] Linder argued that personal property (including slaves) had to be protected. Ficklin tried to convince the judges that the Ordinance of 1787 and the Illinois State Constitution gave freedom to Jane and her children. Ficklin recorded Lincoln's position: "The fact that General Matson had at such a time when he placed a slave on his Illinois farm, publicly declared that he was not placed there for permanent settlement, and that no counter statement had ever been made publicly or privately by him, constituted the web and woof of the argument of Mr. Lincoln, and these facts were plausibly, ingeniously and forcibly presented to the court."[16] After long and detailed presentations, the judges declared that Jane and her children should go free.

The *Matson* case has always been an awkward one for those

14. Weik, p. 755.
15. O. B. Ficklin, " A Pioneer Lawyer." This is a reprint of an article which appeared in a Charleston newspaper in 1885.
16. *Ibid.*

who believe in a mythic Lincoln, since it is rather difficult to explain why the Great Emancipator defended a slave owner. Jesse W. Weik, the first person to write about the affair for a nationwide audience, took the view that Lincoln "*gave his case away!*" and some later biographers followed this approach. Interestingly enough, Jesse Weik, in his article on the Matson case, gave no quotations from Dr. Rutherford on this point, though it is difficult to believe that in his interview with Dr. Rutherford they did not touch on Lincoln's motivation and conduct during the trial. It is more likely that Weik, a Lincoln apologist, did not wish to print Dr. Rutherford's comments. Dr. Rutherford, it is said by members of his family, was highly critical of Lincoln's actions. According to one family story, Dr. Rutherford said that Lincoln arrived at the trial with chains to be used to take the slaves back into captivity. Even if Dr. Rutherford was speaking metaphorically—Lincoln was intent on winning the case for Matson and letting the slaves be returned to Kentucky—this observation would indicate that the doctor did not believe that Lincoln deliberately threw the case away.[17] According to other family accounts, Mr. Weik borrowed all of the doctor's papers concerning the *Matson* case and did not return them. It is not now possible to discover Dr. Rutherford's complete analysis of Lincoln's conduct in this matter.

Dr. Rutherford dealt with the *Matson* case briefly in his letter of October 25, 1847, to John Bowman. Lincoln is not mentioned specifically, for he was not then a national figure. The letter is a particularly reticent one. Why, one might ask, did the doctor not mention his Abolitionist sympathies and the central role he played in the *Matson* case? Answers must be tentative, but Dr. Rutherford was probably unwilling to write openly about the matter because his letters to the Bowmans about Lucinda's death (letters in which he had opened his heart) had caused him much

17. The late Mrs. Eugenia Rutherford Nichols told us this story of Lincoln and the chains. She had the story from her grandmother, Dr. Rutherford's second wife, who attended the Matson trial. It is obvious from Mrs. Nichols' account that her grandparents often spoke of the *Matson* trial and that Dr. Rutherford was much more disenchanted with Lincoln than the published accounts would indicate.

anguish, since Mrs. Bowman held his words against him. Dr. Rutherford, it seems most likely, did not wish to argue the merits of Abolitionism with the rather conservative John Bowman. Too, the Bowman family was seemingly procrastinating in the settlement of an inheritance due the infant John Rutherford, and Dr. Rutherford may not have wished to emphasize to the Bowmans the financial risks he subjected himself to in espousing Abolitionism.

After the trial, Dr. Rutherford told Weik that "Matson left the country, crossed the Wabash river on his way to Kentucky, evaded his creditors, and *never paid Lincoln his fee*." Dr. Rutherford also told Weik that the day following the trial, Lincoln had breakfast, then "mounted on his old gray mare, ruefully set out for the next county on the circuit. As he threw across the animal's back his saddlebags, filled with soiled linen and crumpled court papers, and struck out across the 'measureless prairie,' he gave no further sign, if he experienced it, of any regret because, as a lawyer, he had upheld the case of the strong against the weak."[18]

The same day that Lincoln left Charleston, Ashmore returned the freed slaves to Oakland by wagon, but Dr. Rutherford rode ahead and arrived first. McIntrye described the scene: "As Dr. Rutherford was dismounting from his horse [in Oakland] old Anthony saw him and came breathless to him for the news of the result of the trial, which being told him he went double quick in his old gig tearing down the road out in the country, and Ashmore afterward stated that it was 'worth a horse' to have seen the jubilee. As soon as Anthony came in sight he began to shout and sing, and at the same time his wife began on the same strain. They sang and laughed and prayed and hugged one another all at the same time. Their joy was indescribable; it knew no bounds. No wonder, poor things, their redemption was now complete. They were in a free state, no longer slaves, but free, in all ways which that word implies."[19]

Immediately after the trial, Anthony Bryant decided to take

18. Weik, p. 757.
19. McIntyre.

his family away from the scene of their troubles. Perhaps he feared that Jane and the children would be kidnapped and returned to Kentucky. Whatever the reasons, he sold his few goods and Dr. Rutherford and Ashmore raised additional money to transport the Bryants to Liberia. One of the contributors was William Herndon, Lincoln's law partner.[20]

The story of the Bryants, though, had an ending which Dr. Rutherford and Ashmore could not have foreseen. Elder S. S. Ball of the Colored Baptist Association of Illinois was sent to Liberia in the late spring of 1848 to look into conditions there. He saw the Bryants in Monrovia: "They were truly in a deplorable situation. . . . They were placed on the outskirts of the town, and were all going through the fever. They all shed tears on seeing me, and began to represent their distress. They informed me that they had upon one occasion sent all around Monrovia to beg a chicken, and could not get one. . . . The old gentleman wanted the Three Kentucky Delegates and myself to . . . bring him and his family back to the U. States . . . but this was out of our power."[21] There is no indication that Dr. Rutherford and Ashmore ever learned of the plight of the Bryants in Liberia.

Dr. Rutherford's participation in the efforts to free Jane and her children brought him into conflict with his community. Attorney Ficklin says that there were thirty-three Abolitionists in Coles County at the time of the Matson trial and that "Clay Whigs and Jackson Democrats were very chary, while candidates for office, in being seen in the company of or holding communion with this sect, for the slightest taint of abolitionists would blight all prospects for election." During the trial, Ficklin went on, Rutherford and Ashmore were "denounced as harborers of runaway negroes in escaping from their master. . . . The sympathies of the goundlings and the rabble were for Matson, and it was only now and then that men of intelligence and sober sense would be heard to declare that the negroes were entitled to a fair hearing."[22]

20. Weik, p. 758.
21. Paul M. Angle, "Aftermath of the Matson Slave Case," pp. 148–49.
22. Ficklin, "A Pioneer Lawyer."

McIntyre had noted that there was sympathy for Jane and her children after the first trial. Dr. Rutherford was probably not too concerned about the changing public views, for he was following his conscience. He knew, too, on a practical level, that he was the only well-trained physician in Oakland, and a seriously ill proslavery Oaklander had no choice but to call for the Abolitionist doctor.

Dr. Rutherford remained a man of astute judgments, and when he was an old man he made these observations about Lincoln and the *Matson* case:

> Of the subsequent history of Mr. Lincoln we are all familiar, and while I would detract nothing commendable therefrom, still justice demands that it be said that neither his speeches nor his conduct at and during this litigation was worthy of his name and subsequent fame. Mr. Linder, as an old time member of the Coles County bar, was an orator certainly remarkable. Charley Constable, who was afterwards the honored judge of the circuit court in this county, was retained to defend against the 'black laws' suit, was the best educated lawyer at the bar, the only one who had ever attended a law school. He, with his able assistant Col. Ficklin, threw the case out of court, and with it ended the operation of the so-called 'black laws' in this county. Of Mr. Ficklin little need be added to what has been already written. At a ripe old age he was gathered to his fathers. It was my privilege, with many other old friends to pass by his coffin, to look upon his familiar face, and to see him with due honors placed in the ground. That night the court convened and held a memorial service to his honor. I sat by and heard with pleasure the many good and kind things said about him by his fellow members of the bar, but strange to say, the best and greatest event of his life was not mentioned. They did not know perhaps that in his last journey, he would reach St. Peter's gate, bearing as a ticket pass the shackles of five slaves, for the good apostle to look upon and honor.[23]

For decades following the *Matson* trial, Dr. Hiram Rutherford

23. McIntyre. McIntyre seems to have been quoting from an article by Dr. Rutherford on the *Matson* case, though such an article has not been found.

led an active life as physician, husband, father, farmer, and businessman. He was Oakland's leading citizen, a figure of stability in an unstable world. He saw the Civil War, Reconstruction, economic depressions, droughts, and natural calamities. As useful as it might be, we cannot offer a complete life and times of Dr. Rutherford; what we have offered are vivid and illuminating fragments of his life and times in Illinois from 1840 to 1848.

Bibliography
Index

BIBLIOGRAPHY

Books and Articles

ANGLE, PAUL M. "Aftermath of the Matson Slave Case." *Abraham Lincoln Quarterly* 3(1944):146–49.

———. Editor of *Life on the Circuit with Lincoln*, by Henry C. Whitney. Caldwell, Idaho: Caxton Printers, 1940.

Annual Announcement of Lectures, &c. in Jefferson Medical College, for the Session of 1837–8. Philadelphia: A. Waldie, 1837.

BATEMAN, NEWTON, and SELBY, PAUL. *Illinois Historical and Douglas County Biographical*. Chicago: Munsell, 1910.

BAUER, EDWARD LOUIS. *Doctors Made in America*. Philadelphia: Lippincott, 1963.

BOWDEN, HENRY WARNER. *Dictionary of American Religious Biography*. Westport, Conn.: Greenwood Press, 1977.

BUTLER, JOSEPH T. *American Antiques, 1800–1900*. New York: Odyssey Press, 1965.

COLEMAN, CHARLES H. *Abraham Lincoln and Coles County, Illinois*. New Brunswick, N.J.: Scarecrow Press, 1955.

DUFF, JOHN J. *A. Lincoln: Prairie Lawyer*. New York: Rinehart and Co., 1960.

DUNAWAY, WAYLAND F. *A History of Pennsylvania*. Englewood Cliffs, N.J.: Prentice-Hall, 1964.

FICKLIN, O. B. "A Pioneer Lawyer," *Tuscola Review*, September 7, 1922.

HARDING, WALTER. *The Days of Henry Thoreau*. New York: Knopf, 1965.

History of Coles County, 1876–1976. Dallas: Taylor Publishing Co., 1976.

History of Coles County, Illinois. Chicago: W. Le Baron, Jr., & Co., 1879.

KAUFMAN, MARTIN, *Homeopathy in America: The Rise and Fall of a Medical Heresy*. Baltimore: Johns Hopkins Univ. Press, 1971.

KELLY, HOWARD A., and BURRAGE, WALTER L. *American Medical Biographies*. Baltimore: Norman, Remington Co., 1920.

LAMBERT, MARCUS B. *A Dictionary of Non-English Words of the Pennsylvania-German Dialect*. Lancaster, Pa.: Lancaster Press, 1924.

Bibliography

NORWOOD, WILLIAM FREDERICK. *Medical Education in the United States Before the Civil War*. Philadelphia: Univ. of Pennsylvania Press, 1944.

PEASE, THEODORE CALVIN. *The Frontier State, 1818–1848*. Chicago: A. C. McClurg & Co., 1922.

PICKARD, MADGE E., and BULEY, R. CARLYLE. *The Midwest Pioneer: His Ills, Cures, & Doctors*. New York: Schuman, 1946.

RAWLINGS, ISAAC D. *The Rise and Fall of Disease in Illinois*. Springfield, Ill.: Schnepp & Barnes, 1927.

RICHMOND, PHYLLIS A. "Glossary of Historical Fever Terminology." *Theory and Practice in American Medicine*. New York: Science History Publications, 1976.

ROTHSTEIN, WILLIAN G. *American Physicians in the Nineteenth Century: From Sects to Science*. Baltimore: Johns Hopkins Univ. Press, 1972.

RUSSELL, LORIS S. *A Heritage of Light*. Toronto: Univ. of Toronto Press, 1968.

The Spirit of Independence. Oakland, Ill.: Landmarks, 1972.

STERN, MADELEINE B. *Heads & Headlines: The Phrenological Fowlers*. Norman: University of Oklahoma Press, 1971.

VAN DOREN, MARK. *The Autobiography of Mark Van Doren*. New York: Harcourt, Brace & Co., 1958.

VOIGHT, JOHN W. "A New Geography of Coles County." *Illinois Magazine* 16(1977):17–42.

Weik, Jesse W. "Lincoln and the Matson Negroes, A Vista into the Fugitive Slave Days." *Arena* 17(1897):752–58.

ZEUCH, LUCIUS H. *History of Medical Practice in Illinois*. Chicago: Book Press, 1927.

Manuscript and Unpublished Materials

Private Collection of Austin Rutherford. "The Matson Slave Trial," Oakland *Weekly Ledger*, June 17, 1896 [by P. T. McIntyre].

Private Collection of Nina Rutherford Zimmerman. Letters of Dr. Hiram Rutherford and Lucinda Bowman Rutherford.

Springfield, Illinois. Southern Illinois University School of Medicine, Department of Medical Humanities. "Health and Medicine in Central and Southern Pioneer Illinois" [by J. K. Crellin].

Urbana-Champaign, Illinois. University of Illinois Library. Illinois Historical Survey. "Commodity Prices 1840–1860, Chicago," Dr. Hiram Rutherford's college texts, lecture notes, account books, and his "Jonas Bragg—A Personal Sketch."

Index

Index

Index

Index

Index

Index